A Century of Modern Drawing
from The Museum of Modern Art New York

BERNICE ROSE

Published by British Museum Publications Limited for
THE TRUSTEES OF THE BRITISH MUSEUM
MUSEUM OF FINE ARTS, BOSTON
THE CLEVELAND MUSEUM OF ART

The exhibition was organized under the auspices of The International Council of the Museum of Modern Art, New York.

Illustrated on first page: (top) Seurat, *Stone Breakers, Le Raincy*, cat. no. 182; (bottom) Rosenquist, *White Spot*, cat. no. 171

Illustrated on previous page: Cézanne, *Mercury after Pigalle*, cat. no. 19

Illustrated opposite: Miro, *Statue*, cat. no. 120

© 1982 The Museum of Modern Art, New York. All rights reserved.
ISBN 0 7141 0791 3
Published by British Museum Publications Limited, 46 Bloomsbury Street, London WC1B 3QQ
Designed by Roger Davies
Set in Monophoto Photina and printed in Great Britain by W. S. Cowell Ltd., Ipswich

A Century of Modern Drawing *from The Museum of Modern Art, New York*

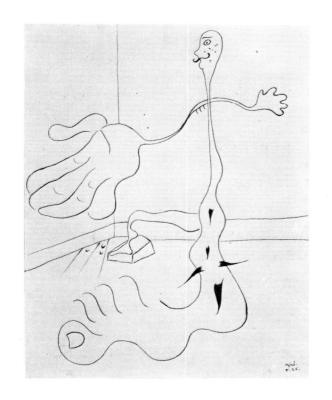

Contents

Foreword

The Museum of Modern Art in New York has given us an unprecedented opportunity to display a substantial cross-section of one of the greatest collections of modern drawing in the world. Our colleagues in the Oriental Antiquities Department have generously made their gallery available for this exhibition, so that we can show works on a considerable scale which are such an important part of twentieth century art. It is the first exhibition held in the British Museum devoted exclusively to modern drawing and we hope it will draw attention to our own interests in a field where we have begun to make significant acquisitions. Above all, it should serve as an inspiration; for the kind of acquisitions The Museum of Modern Art has been making provide us with a fine example of what can be achieved through enlightened patronage and demonstrate that a great deal could still be achieved with a serious and imaginative commitment to the building of a twentieth century collection.

John Rowlands KEEPER, *Department of Prints and Drawings*

cknowledgments

The preparation of such a large and complex exhibition is always the work of many people, and in this case, thanks must be shared by both the staff of the British Museum, London, and the staff of The Museum of Modern Art, New York. Frances Carey, Assistant Keeper in the Department of Prints and Drawings at The British Museum deserves the major share of the credit for the exhibition. From its inception, at her request, to the selection and arrangement the work has been one of close collaboration between Miss Carey and myself; the exhibition as it stands is a joint venture. I would like to thank her and John Rowlands, Keeper of the Department of Prints and Drawings, and the Director of the British Museum, Dr David Wilson, for making this exhibition possible.

In New York, I would like to thank John Elderfield, Director of the Department of Drawings for his encouragement of the project and his support throughout its preparation. Beatrice Kernan, Curatorial Assistant in the Department of Drawings, has been an invaluable and tireless assistant. Ms Kernan and Monique Imbert, Research Cataloguer, have worked hard during a particularly trying period as the collection was being relocated, to pursue endless details and provide photographs for the catalogue despite constant disruptions. Monawee Richards, Researcher, deserves special thanks for her compilation of the artists' biographies. I am particularly indebted to the editor of this publication, Harriet Schoenholz Bee, for her constant encouragement and support throughout the writing of the text and for her expert editorial supervision of the text and catalogue to completion. Riva Castleman, Director of the Department of Prints and Illustrated Books, was a patient adviser and gave much valuable advice on prints and printmaking techniques.

I would also like to thank Waldo Rasmussen, Director of the International Program of The Museum, and Elizabeth Streibert, Assistant Director for their co-ordinating all phases of the project to see that it, indeed, happened. Thanks are also due to The International Council of The Museum and its Chairman and President, Prinz Franz von Bayern and Mrs Alfred R. Stern for the Council's support of the project.

In addition, thanks are due to all of those who worked over the years to build The Museum's drawing collection, among them Paul J. Sachs, Alfred H. Barr, Jr., and William S. Lieberman.

Finally, with deep appreciation, I would like to acknowledge the numerous donors who have been so generous over the years and without whom no collection at all would exist.

Bernice Rose CURATOR, *Department of Drawings,*
The Museum of Modern Art, New York

Preface

When The Museum of Modern Art first opened its doors in November 1929, it owned but a single drawing and a group of prints. Now, shortly after the Museum's fiftieth Anniversary, its drawing collection numbers approximately 6,000 works on paper, ranging from works in the traditional drawing mediums of pencil, ink, and charcoal to those in oil, watercolour, gouache, pastel, and collage as well as certain newly-invented mediums. This exhibition is presented both as a selection of works of particular quality, indicating the richness of the collection, and as a review of modern draughtsmanship, showing its diversity and historical development.

When the Museum of Modern Art was founded it contained no facilities for the separate collection and study of drawings. Such works were gradually acquired either because they served as studies for paintings or sculptures the Museum owned or because they filled important lacunae in the Museum's historical collection as a whole. While these functions continued (and continue) to be served by the drawing collection, it gradually evolved an autonomous status with its principle being to create an independent historical and qualitative overview of modern art in works on paper.

Alfred H. Barr, Jr., the Museum's first director, was largely instrumental in forming the drawing collection. With the support of Barr's former teacher, Professor Paul J. Sachs, one of the seven founder-trustees of the Museum, and through the particular generosity of three other founder-trustees, Lillie P. Bliss, Abby Aldrich Rockefeller, and A. Conger Goodyear, and of John S. Newberry, the collection grew steadily in size. It was not, however, until 1964 that the Museum inaugurated galleries especially devoted to the exhibition of drawings and prints from its collections, naming these galleries in honour of Professor Sachs. And it was not until 1971 that the Museum established a separate curatorial Department of Drawings, directed by William S. Lieberman, under whose auspices the collection grew rapidly in size, with many important additions, chief among them The Joan and Lester Avnet Collection, which was itself formed with the needs of the Museum specifically in mind. Since Mr Lieberman's retirement from the Museum at the end of 1979, the current director has pursued the idea of a historically synoptic collection of significant quality with the assistance of many generous donors, especially from the Museum's Committee on Drawings. In the spring of 1983, expanded facilities for the study and exhibition of drawings, including a new study centre and galleries devoted exclusively to works on paper, will be provided as part of the Museum's enlarged premises, due to be completed at that date.

It is, in the first place, because of the disruptions in programming necessarily caused by the Museum's reconstruction that it can make available an exhibition of such unprecedented scope as that documented in this catalogue. Substantial selections from the drawing collection have previously been shown in circulating exhibitions in 1947, 1960 and 1974. This exhibition, however, comprises certainly the largest and most important survey yet mounted. There are inevitably a number of key works that cannot be included because of their fragility, and others that have been excluded in order to keep the exhibition of manageable size. And, of course, any selection from a collection of around 6,000 works is necessarily a partial and personal interpretation of that collection by those who chose the exhibition. Additionally, certain specialised aspects of the collection, including its Theatre Arts material and its vast holdings in the work of such artists as Dubuffet, Kupka and Feininger, are given only minimal representation. But all that said, the exhibition presents both the most representative and most significant selection from the collection that has yet been shown outside The Museum of Modern Art itself. The Museum warmly welcomes the opportunity it affords to share these master works from its collection with The British Museum, London, the Cleveland Museum of Art and the Museum of Fine Arts, Boston, and with the audiences that these institutions serve.

The conception of the exhibition, and the principal credit for it, belongs to Bernice Rose, Curator in the Department of Drawings at The Museum of Modern Art, and Frances Carey, Assistant Keeper in the Department of Prints and Drawings at The British Museum. They recognised that the period of The Museum of Modern Art's expansion offered a unique opportunity to show, for the very first time, work from its collection at a great museum that was itself beginning to collect in the modern field. I am grateful to Mrs Rose and Ms Carey for their organisation of this often complicated project, as well as to the many people who assisted them and who are listed by Mrs Rose in her own acknowledgments. Here, however, I must thank John Rowlands, Keeper of the Department of Prints and Drawings at The British Museum, and Dr David Wilson, Director of that Museum, for their enthusiastic support of the exhibition; also Sherman Lee, Director of the Cleveland Museum of Art, and Jan Fontein, Director of the Museum of Fine Arts, Boston, for their wanting to share in this very exciting enterprise.

This exhibition is an occasion both for celebration and for evaluation. It celebrates a collection of modern works on paper that is often considered as unparalleled; The Museum of Modern Art is proud to be able to present an exhibition of such scope and quality. At the same time, it allows evaluation on at least three very basic levels: first, the weaknesses as well as strengths of the collection become particularly evident in surveys of this kind, reminding us not only of what has been achieved but of what remains to be done. Second, the history of modern drawing itself is presented as a subject of evaluation, allowing study of its own strengths and weaknesses in addition to its variety and its development. And third, as seen in three major institutions whose terms of reference are far broader than that of modern art, this exhibition allows for the evaluation of modern works on paper in the context established by earlier art, and by the standards set by that art for the century of modern drawing shown here.

John Elderfield DIRECTOR, *Department of Drawings,*
The Museum of Modern Art

Introduction

The Museum's drawing collection begins with the year 1881, an arbitrary place to begin and one based on the fortunes of collecting, but appropriate nevertheless because it brings us immediately into confrontation with two of the crucial issues of the modern movement. These are the release of colour from conventional contour drawing in Impressionist painting (bringing with it the isolation of the paint stroke, the tendency to abstraction, and the focus on the picture plane as flat) and the loosening of traditional linear perspective as the means of structuring pictorial space.

By going outdoors and painting, rather than sketching, before nature, the colourists had temporarily won the old academic dispute between line and colour expressed in the academic maxim 'line does not exist in nature'. Following Impressionism, drawing had to be realigned with colour, which had become the dominant means of pictorial expression. The unbroken course from the nude study (*académie*) and the draped figure or study from nature (*étude*), and the concurrent study of perspective drawing, to the compositional study or 'artificial pictorial scheme', to the *ébauche*, to the painting itself was open to reinterpretation and rearrangement. The initial restudy of one-point linear perspective in the work of Paul Cézanne, Vincent van Gogh, Paul Gauguin and Georges Pierre Seurat led to its replacement by a new system of linear construction developed in the work of Henri Matisse, Georges Braque and Pablo Picasso, from 1906 on, culminating in Braque's and Picasso's *papier collé* of 1912. Line, no longer responsible for perspective projection through the imagined window of the Renaissance conception of 'real' space, was reorganised by Braque and Picasso as a new structural element on the surface of the picture plane. The new illusionism of material surfaces, originally projected by tactile means in Impressionism, was given structural definition. In 1912 a new strategy for pictorial construction based on a new linear structural system clearly replaced the old. Even before the introduction of *papier collé* in 1912, from 1910 on, one element of the new structure, its organisation of the picture surface into planar areas — the result of geometric analysis and its concomitant fracturing of form — was in widespread use.

It is in this context that Cézanne's late watercolours began the history of modern drawing. Originally Cézanne had wished to reorganise the dispersed visual sensations of Impressionism and return them to the construction of solid objects in space; it is paradoxical, therefore, that his late style once more dissolved the solidity of these objects. The perception of form became essentially a function of reflection, sensations of light reflecting off objects projected through the atmosphere to the retina. In painting, these sensations of light were rendered in colour (in the last two years of his life Cézanne spoke of the sensations of colour that *give* light). In order to organise these light sensations to depict solid objects, drawing had to be reintroduced to painting. But Cézanne 'wished to return to the object without abandoning the Impressionist aesthetic which takes nature for its mode . . ., without any other guide to nature than its immediacy, without delineating the contour, without framing the colour by drawing, without composing the perspective of the picture itself.'[1]

Cézanne increasingly regarded drawing as a function of colour construction and in the late 1870s[2] in his watercolours set about creating a system for reorganising drawing according to colour differentiations, or modulations; line was accommodated, but: 'Pure drawing is an abstrac-

1. Maurice Merleau-Ponty, 'Cézanne's Doubt', trans. Sonia Brownell, *Art and Literature* (Lausanne, Spring 1965), p. 110.

2. Lawrence Gowing, 'The Logic of Organized Sensations', in *Cézanne: The Late Work* (New York: The Museum of Modern Art, 1977), p. 56. I am indebted at many points in the section on Cézanne to this essay.

tion, drawing and colour are not distinct points, everything in nature is coloured.'[3] By the late 1890s his system of organised colour perceptions, his colour patches and dark lines, had become his chief pictorial method. He was thought to have abandoned drawing but told Emile Bernard:

> 'Drawing and painting are no longer different factors, as one paints, one draws: the more harmony there is in the colours the more precise the drawing becomes. When the colour is at its richest, the form is at its fullest. Contrasts and harmonies of tones, there is the secret of drawing and modeling.'[4]

The effect of superimposed patches of transparent, pure colour is an invention of Cézanne's that he called *petites sensations*: varicoloured shadows rendered as the product of light reflecting off the local colours of objects and mixing with the ambient light. These *petites sensations* required expression and organisation: 'Art is personal perception. This perception I place in feeling and I ask of feeling that it should organise it into a work.'[5]

Cézanne, synthesising drawing and painting in the watercolours, took advantage of a convention of drawing that constitutes its chief peculiarity as a discipline, one previously closed to painting with its conventional notions of finish: he used reserve areas of the white sheet, areas left blank, to stand for light. Thus he could, in a sense, parallel nature's light. It was no longer necessary to see light in painting as coming from a source outside the picture. His aim was to create art as 'a harmony parallel to nature' by making colour contrasts the internal life of art and the white sheet nature's light.

Watercolour satisfied his need for a medium in which the senses and intelligence could work together to 'paint matter in the act of taking form, the birth of order through spontaneous organisation'.[6] Its speed of execution and its transparency guaranteed that the structure in formation was always apparent and, above all, that the white sheet could stand for pure light, indeed for the object itself. The system developed in the watercolours not only dissolved the objects into ambient space, but by so doing 'eliminated the material substance that remained the subject of the oil pictures',[7] rendering the watercolour system itself sufficient in many respects, thereby creating the famous 'crisis of finish' in Cézanne's later work:

> 'Now being old, nearly seventy years, the sensations of colour, which give light, are for me the reason for the abstractions that do not allow me to cover my canvas entirely or to pursue the delimitation of objects where their points of contact are fine and delicate; from which it results that my image or picture is incomplete. . . . Otherwise the planes fall on top of one another, [as in styles] which circumscribe the contours with a black line, a fault that must be fought at all costs. But nature, if consulted, gives us the means of attaining this end.'[8]

The subject of the pictures became the depiction of a profuse universe in the constant process of creating itself as a unified structure; nothing is given, the space and the objects constantly discover and reconstruct one another, there is no *a priori* system of perspective, the transparent colour patch itself usurps the place of the object so that each brush stroke must 'contain the air, the light, the object, the construction, the character, the drawing, the style'.[9] The urgency to retain the freshness of the original perception that one feels in Cézanne belongs to the con-

3. Cézanne, quoted by Léo Larguier, 'Extraits de Le Dimanche avec Paul Cézanne', reprinted in *Conversations avec Cézanne*, ed. P. M. Doran (Macula, 1978), p. 16, no. XXVIII.

4. Cézanne, quoted by Emile Bernard in *Conversations avec Cézanne*, p. 63.

5. Cézanne, quoted in Merleau-Ponty, 'Cézanne's Doubt', p. 111.

6. Ibid.

7. Gowing, 'Organized Sensations', p. 56.

8. Ibid., p. 68.

9. Merleau-Ponty, 'Cézanne's Doubt', p. 110.

vention of drawing, but each picture was built up over more than one session by Cézanne, who laboured to retain the freshness as he laboured to synthesise a myriad of sensations to one essential one and to the general structural conception.

In *Foliage* (1895–1900) (pl. 11) it is possible to see how the blank sheet stands for the leaves themselves: the point closest to the viewer, the *point culminant*, is rendered as the point of greatest reflection and stands for the object itself. Embracing the *point culminant* and receding from it on each side are the shadows, colour patches representing reflected light, rendered sequentially according to a system of colour modulation, the key to which is the green leaves. Light from different sources will be differently coloured, no area of a flat surface will be always the same colour, because of the changing angle of vision. Patches recede into deepest shadow where, no longer attached to the object, they settle into the interstices between figures (where they tend to fuse with adjacent objects). There, joined by the vibrating contour lines which act simultaneously as a line of separation and a connective, they become part of the overall structure in a system of rhythmically accented parallel and radiating linear sequences across the picture.

In *Mont Sainte-Victoire Seen from Les Lauves* (1902–1906)[10] and *Rocky Ridge above Le Château Noir* (1895–1900) one can see how the contour lines form an overall structural system that operates as a parallel to the system of colour patches but ties the individual forms in a network that secures them to the surface plane and the edges of the sheet. An important component of the drawing system is the *points culminants*, rendered as though each object were seen from the front; the reserve whites of the *points* unite with the reserve ground in other parts of the composition to assure the homogeneity of ground and object. The system of drawing through open and closed contours, rendered as colour patches and lines, gradually defining objects, results in forms fusing to one another and to adjacent space, only to be broken: a system of opposed perceptions rendered as simultaneous (called *passages*) that guarantees a homogeneous pictorial structure.

Cézanne's work represents the watershed at which perceptual perspective, which had appeared at various other times, began to dominate the structure of art. He arrived at a new perspective, a perspective of seeing (later Matisse would have perspective of feeling). The whole composition is rendered as though the spatial plane were slightly convex; Cézanne noted, with regard to flat surfaces, that 'bodies seen in space are all convexes'.[11] The rendering of space itself as curved corresponds to the curving plane of vision. As explained by Cézanne, as eyes move across a surface their angle of vision changes with each shift in point of view; they record not a continuous flat surface but one subtly curved away from the *point culminant* on each side into convexity. Perspective is created by the multiplicity of these points of view; just as the movement of objects in space is established by the multiplicity of their contours, so each is frozen into place, fixed by each stroke of the brush, hence the reason for the constant *point culminant*. This fixing at a particular point arrests the movement towards linear perspective, creating a more dynamic, compressed space. In organising the picture, the eye is referred into perspective space but also across the surface to the edges of the composition, receding slightly from the edge of the sheet, which corresponds to the edge of our curved field of vision. The constant unifying factor is the light of the white sheet shining

10. Collection Mr and Mrs David Rockefeller, New York.

11. Quoted in Gowing, 'Organized Sensations', p. 57.

through the compositional field. The condition of finish appropriate to drawing was the condition of the new painting. Drawing itself changed from a system of making a flat surface into a three-dimensional world to one with which the artist was free to reconstruct the world as he saw fit. Eventually a new pictorial strategy emerged that was directed towards making the three-dimensional world into a flat picture.

Georges Pierre Seurat's drawing represents a wholly different accommodation of drawing to colour. Seurat, too, evolved a synthesis of sequential and immediate perceptions, fixed in time, as one of the conditions for a new pictorial structure. His drawings are amazing conceptualisations of the relationship of gradation and contrast to colour harmony (of tone to colour). Rendered in velvety tonalities in black conté crayon, they are finished works; while they suggest all the sensations of light and tone normally felt in colour rendering, they are both independent works functioning on the one hand as contrasts to the paintings, and on the other, as analogies to them. In light the mix of all colours creates white; in solid matter pigment, the mix of all colours, creates black. Seurat's paintings fracture the black of the drawings into its component colour parts; the paintings aspire to the condition of light, that is, they mix optically towards white. From 1880 to 1882 Seurat concentrated exclusively on drawing in black conté crayon. Doing no painting in colour, he studied the problems of value and contrast, reflection and interpenetration, and the balance of light and dark masses in a series of drawings in which, having already abandoned the contour drawing of Ingres, he gradually eliminated linear drawing for tonal rendering of form.

Seurat had learned drawing in the academic tradition of Ingres — toned, hard-contour drawing; the ideal form was sculptural, the ideal drawing treated the human figure like a piece of sculpture, an idea that remained with him despite the virtual elimination of linear drawing. During this period, despite the fact that his intention must have been to restudy drawing primarily in order to master a new conception of form before beginning to paint, Seurat seems to have arrived at his original and mature conception of drawing as not only independent of and analogous to painting, but one in which the drawing is a fragment of the larger world that constitutes the painting; by virtue of their intensity, Seurat's drawings magnify the microcosm to the macrocosm.

In 1883 Seurat began to paint in his famous pointillist style, interposing the immaculately finished black drawings as a means of study between more broadly brushed outdoor colour sketches in oil and finished painting. *Stone Breakers, Le Raincy* (c. 1881) shows a relatively early stage of Seurat's drawing, overall-hatching beginning to replace linear outline, except for figures. The sheet is already the light source, and interpenetration and reflection are already an important subject. By 1884, in the studies for *A Sunday Afternoon on the Island of 'La Grand Jatte'* (1884–6),[12] such as *Lady with a Parasol* (1884–5) (fig. 2), there is a distinct technical change signaling a new formal conception. The form emerges from the ground as the conté crayon, used broadly, reduces Seurat's drawing unit to the little particles of matter that cling to the rough surface of the drawing sheet (chosen because its texture was like that of canvas), the densities varying in response to the pressure of his hand. The black elements are undifferentiated, the form emerges as a consequence of contrasting dense masses against lighter ones, creating an impression of the convergence and divergence of particles in move-

12. The Art Institute of Chicago. Helen Birch Bartlett Memorial Collection.

13. John Rewald, *Post-Impressionism: From van Gogh to Gauguin* (New York: The Museum of Modern Art, 1962), p. 80.

14. Meyer Schapiro, 'Seurat', in *Modern Art: 19th and 20th Centuries* (New York: George Braziller, 1978), p. 108.

15. According to Henri Dorra, Seurat's proportion for *Le Cirque* (1890–91, unfinished, Louvre, Paris) is based on the Golden Section, 'that division of a line or proportion of a geometrical figure in which the smaller dimension is to the greater as the greater is to the whole'. This was an ideal proportion according to Neoplatonic philosophy. The connection suggests that Seurat's scientific structure was embedded in Neoplatonism insofar as the Neoplatonic physical world was seen as emanating from the divine being, (to paraphrase Erwin Panofsky, quoting Ficino, Plotinus and Suger in *Renaissance and Renascences in Western Art*, pp. 183–8). According to Abbot Suger, the artist is charged with the task of providing 'manual' guidance that 'enables the human mind to ascend through all things to the cause of all things'. Neoplatonic philosophy (here Panofsky quotes Ernst Gombrich) 'abolished all borderlines between the sacred and profane', and 'succeeded in opening up to secular art emotional spheres that had hitherto been the preserve of religious worship'. We can imagine Seurat's work as lit from within by this radiant light: science as metaphysics. We can also make the connection between the drawing and the idea, the conceptual principle of the work preceding its physical execution.

16. James Johnson Sweeney, 'Plastic Redirections in 20th Century Painting', in *Studies of Meaning in Art* (New York: Arno Press, 1972), p. 9.

ment. Edges vibrate reciprocally: the dark glow lighter, the light darker. The method for composing the paintings was additive but subordinate to a general organisational preconception of angles and curves, tones and colours. The composition was studied in fragments, coloured studies on the spot and black drawings in the studio; area by area, accumulating images augmented and clarified the original conception and were subordinated to it and to a developing final overall structure of linear analogies and oppositions.

As detail studies for figures and compositional areas of the whole, the drawings served a double purpose: as intermediaries between the more broadly rendered and spontaneous outdoor colour sketch, refining the touch and eliminating the spontaneous and particular, generalising the figures and objects into simple, almost geometric, forms, and as studies in the relationship of tone to density – the proper balance of 'light, shade, local colour, interaction of colours'.[13] Drawing became part of a scientific system for rationalising each component of the pictorial means.

One aspect of this system is to use drawing to recycle the first impression before nature to a new beginning point in art, to the origins of form coalescing out of matter. Form emerges out of the broken ground, the myriad and varicoloured strokes coalescing according to patterns of light and dark to create the edges of the forms, defining them and modulating volume. It is as though the world were formed out of little particles of matter given to our eyes as form through the reflection of light rendered by the colour patches. The scale of values in the black drawings suggested the complete colour harmony: Seurat had only to establish the local hue and apply his system of colour contrasts and analogies to translate the appropriate modulations. This probably accounts for the intense colour sensation of the black drawings. The accumulation and accommodation of individual pieces of data from study to drawing and drawing to study progressively synthesised the impressions, gathered over a long period of time, to one essential one, frozen in time in the paintings. Thus the paintings are reflexive in more than one sense; they are also images of memory in contrast to the relatively more immediate observations of the drawings.

Meyer Schapiro notes that in his involvement with new theory, as in much else, Seurat is essentially modern. A 'sympathetic vision of the mechanical in the constructed environment',[14] is echoed in his art by the reduction of his means to standard elements and the exposure, in the final form, of the working structural members.

In Seurat's late works line returns as an element, not drawn line – line given by contrast – but line nevertheless, in the organisation of the canvas according to a geometric system of lines, verticals, horizontals, and diagonals, based on the golden section.[15] 'The human figure, as well as other natural objects were, for him, first and always, elements of an architecture. Every natural object offered a play of volume and interval to be tied up intimately with the total picture space. Inessentials were eliminated. Broken contours were avoided. And nature, in the making of a picture, was despoiled of any superficial sensual charms that might distract the attention from the total architectonic effect. . . . The physiology of Seurat's world was completely dominated by the hollow of his canvas'.[16] Cézanne had told Emile Bernard that nature should be organised according to the sphere, cylinder, and cone. This concept of analogising simple geometric figures, adapted from the academic method, became an important organising principle for the first generation of artists of the twentieth century.

Seurat's drawings however, like those of his contemporary, Odilon Redon, remain the ideal of every colourist: black drawings that suggest all the nuances of colour rendering. Redon's drawings were also conceived as finished work, and he, too, worked at first exclusively in black, although in charcoal. His subjects, which he claimed to have observed in nature, were extrapolated out of nature by fantasy; he was initially an illustrator and continued to be inspired by literary sources, as in *The Masque of the Red Death* (1883) (fig. 4), based on a story by Edgar Allan Poe. As his style evolved, like Seurat, he tended to integrate outline drawing to the evocation of form out of a primordial ground of black, by massing tone, and to picking out forms and highlights by erasure. His turn to colour drawing in pastel in the late 1890s coincided with the increasing dominance of colour as the century ended and marked his emergence as a 'modern' artist.

In the meantime, however, Gauguin and van Gogh worked out new accommodations of contour drawing to colour. As early as 1886 van Gogh wrote, 'Colour expresses something by itself', but noted about traditional Dutch painting that 'one of the most beautiful things has been the painting of black which nevertheless has light in it'.[17] The rendering of the 'black which nevertheless has light in it' became the task of van Gogh's drawings, which, like Seurat's, operate both as studies and independent tonal essays. Van Gogh's painting style is a direct translation of his touch in drawing. In *Hospital Corridor at Saint-Rémy* (1889–90) (pl. 1) his painting strokes are isolated from the mass and can be easily identified and compared with the reed pen strokes of the drawing in *Street at Saintes-Maries* (1888) (fig. 1).

Van Gogh's mature drawing style, at its most radical, is abstracted from the great Dutch landscapists and Jean Francois Millet. Continuous outline drawing is eliminated, and van Gogh adopts instead the seventeenth-century Dutch masters' device of repeating short linear strokes detached from contours for shading, reducing these to a coded system. The contour of each form is reduced to a sign for itself; each form is given a characteristic mark which becomes its sign. Millet contributes the conceptions of colouristic interpenetration and reflection, which van Gogh interprets. Instead of variations in tone given by one kind of touch with one kind of means (Millet's dry crayon and pastel), van Gogh gives us the touch and pressure of different instruments and mediums, wet and dry — pen and ink, crayon and pencil — for different textural, and therefore different colouristic, effects: opaque, translucent, soft, sharp, fine, thick, short, long, dotted, and so on. The different accents of the strokes are stimuli that provoke a variety of kinetic responses in the eye, producing different sensations of light, corresponding to sensations of colour in his painting. Van Gogh renders line as virtually a conceptual abstraction (and in this he influences Piet Mondrian), but the repetition of similar marks in series re-establishes the descriptive function of certain of his marks: thus the phrasing of curved lines establishes trees, while little straight lines become grass, and we understand that the truly non-descriptive points represent a generalised notion for texture on a flat surface. The diverse marks are organised into contained, shifting planar areas, generally opposed by more organic and frontal foreground masses. Distance is given by the size of the mark, while the scale and rhythm of the repetitive phrasing — the density — of

17. John Russell, *The Meanings of Modern Art*, vol. 1 (New York: The Museum of Modern Art, 1974) p. 40.

the marks establishes the specific tonality of each area. Each plane is defined by an implicit linear structure which organises the whole composition. With linear perspective at its moment of greatest danger, van Gogh insists on it as an expressive device exaggerating its almost inexorable recession while constantly interrupting it, as in *Hospital Corridor*, by organising the composition into shifting tilting planes, here reflecting his anxiety. In effect, this exaggeration reverses the role of perspective, and the tilting planes rush forward towards us so that both texture and perspective now assert the picture as object. In this, van Gogh's anxiety seems both personal and expressive of the times, one of real change in the existing structure of art for which he is partially responsible.

Gauguin left very few drawings, but in *Jacob Meyer de Haan* (1889) we can see that his style was one of radically simplified contour drawing — that is, drawing that does not stop for details — worked in concert with broad, shifting planes rendered in homogeneous, artificial colour. The effect of this radically simplified drawing and homogeneously coloured forms is to establish figures and ground on the same plane, rendering figures and objects as two-dimensional, while radically foreshortening and tilting the planes, stressing surface. Gauguin's insistence on continuous decorative contour, whether established by preliminary underdrawing to indicate colour contrasts or by outline drawing on top of the colour as a virtually independent means of expression, set him apart technically from the 'realists', those who, like Cézanne, held observation before nature as the primary task of art. Gauguin's style moves from art to nature and back. He wrote, 'Art is an abstraction; I derive this abstraction from nature while dreaming before it'.[18]

On examination, one suspects that despite his rebellious attitude the root of Gauguin's style was in academic convention: the common element of the popular primitive or exotic styles that interested him was the pre-existent artifice of similar linear systems. The academy took line for granted as a convention of art; it was a language for imitation. 'One suspects that a result of academic training was to conceive of reality as no more than an assemblage of surfaces that were immediately translatable, thanks to this preconceived schemata, by conventional "signs"'.[19] These signs were not simply the elements of the figure reduced to analogous forms. They were the 'separable components of the drawing system itself — contour, hatching, shading — and were evidently thought of at one time as an autonomous aesthetic so that drawing after the life model was thought of in terms of its constitutive vocabulary'[20] — a 'language' of drawing itself. (The signs were conceived as conventions of draughtsmanship, used to transcribe the three-dimensional subject to flat drawing. In studying first from the flat, the student learned that the various forms of the body could be reduced to a system of ellipses that related eyes to breasts, breasts to limbs, and extended the system from eyes to still-life forms. The same conventions could be extended to studies from the three-dimensional cast and from there to the life study — where they became Cézanne's study of nature according to the sphere, cylinder, and cone.) 'The organisation or manipulation of elements within the matrix became the artist's principle task. A reality in itself, then, the language of art lent itself to the kind of analysis to which the philosophers subjected natural reality, too, and we can view it as the visual counterpart of mental systems and perspectives used by experts in other fields to order and contain the reality studied.'[21] Thus we realise

18. Gauguin, quoted in Rewald, *Post-Impressionism*, p. 196.

19. Pierre Rosenberg, 'Academic Life Drawing in 18th Century France', in *Eighteenth Century French Life Drawing* (Princeton, N.J.: Princeton University Press, 1977), p. 35.

20. Ibid.

21. Ibid'

that the exploration of the reality of the latter part of the nineteenth and twentieth centuries became this exploration of the language of art itself (and Cézanne's explorations before nature are seen in a new light).

More immediately, Gauguin can be said to have conserved the mode of contour drawing for the French tradition by a reinterpretation of this convention. Subjecting Ingres's elegant, radical contours to the more immediately expressive reality of less refined styles, Gauguin circumvents Ingres and assumes a primitive version of Gothic enclosure drawing by adopting the style of the contemporary Breton woodblock, a popular derivation from earlier prototypes. It is rougher, with a less elegant line than its progenitor, and, like the much more elegant Japanese woodcut which also had a decisive influence on Gauguin, represents three-dimensional objects as flat decorative areas. The two different versions of this mode of cursive enclosure drawing, one rough and the other elegant, reinforce one another; these, together with Gauguin's own experience in woodblock cutting, create an expressively inflected, tough, and somewhat angular line when compared with the contemporary Art Nouveau line. In Gauguin's art synthetic line is, in fact, the direct result of the woodcut: in the woodcut lines are achieved by cutting away the areas between, creating the line as a line of containment or enclosure which, unless deliberately broken down, is seen as a continuous network, linking forms. The subtracted areas gain in importance as the result of being the focus of containment; they may even be perceived as volumetric. The result of subtracting matter to create the line is to leave its outer edges with traces that become inflections of what has been subtracted; thus the line synthesises to itself memories of the lost bodies between, becomes more expressive — colouristic. The tendency is for negative and positive forms to have equal importance, and to be perceived on the same plane, even when the connectives of one line to another are broken and the continuous contour of a single form is emphasised. This kind of line is always independently expressive of any colour used in conjunction with it. When it forms the basic conception of any drawing style. it will always render three-dimensional form as flat and as continuous and interchangeable with its ground.

This method of studying linear structure had the effect of rendering explicit what was implicit in academic teaching. It exposed the system to the eye as an independent structure and made the system itself a means to be manipulated.

For Gauguin, as for Matisse later, the carving away of matter to create line may have provided the means for circumventing the strictures surrounding contour drawing. At any rate, a return to woodcut as a technique or means formed the basis of many drawing styles employing synthetic line in the first two decades of the twentieth century, among them those of André Derain, Wassily Kandinsky, Ernst Ludwig Kirchner, Paul Klee and Matisse.

The effect of this drawing style is to place Gauguin's work in the great decorative tradition, and in this context, he passes this conception of contour drawing into twentieth-century art. It appears most importantly in Matisse's great early decorative composition, *Dance* (1909),[22] as the means for a wholly new pictorial space. Treating contour drawing as an expressive and structural means independent of colour led also to the work of Georges Rouault and the Fauve artists (drawing directly with colour); allied to the German linear tradition,

22. The Museum of Modern Art, New York. Gift of Nelson A. Rockefeller in honour of Alfred H. Barr, Jr.

it underlay German Expressionism as exemplified by the work of Kirchner.

The dispersal of objects by their rendering as light and shadow created for art a crisis of geometric perspective. It became necessary for the artist to develop a new pictorial strategy wherein the reassembled objects could be accommodated to the flat picture plane already implied by Impressionism. The flat surface was to become the reality to which the three dimensional would be accommodated, rather than the other way round; the new terms were to make a flat picture of a three-dimensional world.

The painter's problem became the lack of a single unifying mechanism comparable to perspective. Matisse and Picasso (with Braque) each began an intensive investigation of these problems, keeping a watchful eye on one another. With perspective, the 'automatic pilot'[23] for pictorial composition, seriously undermined, Matisse and then Picasso returned to the study of the nude figure according to the system of analogies taught at the academy and to the implicit conceptions of the academic drawing system.

Matisse contributed the first new spatial proposition, the first space that broke totally with linear perspective and treated the picture plane as a flat surface to which the three-dimensional forms of the world were accommodated. The issue, for Matisse, was his wish to retain the figure as a motif, while also retaining colour which tends to dissolve tactile sensations. The drawing of the figure in linear black outlines as a system of positive enclosures (derived from the academic system of contour drawing) allied to the sense of the total pictorial space as a scheme of positive and negative enclosures became the key to a new pictorial space accommodating these seemingly contradictory wishes. The academic enclosure drawing system permitted Matisse to render form as coloured volume, while keeping it flat to the picture plane.

From 1906 Matisse's pictorial structure is based on the elaboration and manipulation of the system of enclosure drawing described in connection with Gauguin. In using enclosure drawing as a formal tool for structural analogies, it is possible to concentrate on any one, or combination, of its elements as primary or secondary pictorial devices; it is possible to concentrate on description or simplify towards the more abstract and decorative. In his drawings Matisse isolates and explores one aspect of this mode of drawing, rendering the human body as a study in positive enclosures or contours constantly restudied according to all the possible linear and tonal devices, and their variations and combinations, available to the sophisticated academically trained draughtsman. Matisse, however, not only restudies but reinvents traditional draughtsmanship with each approach to his subject.

Matisse's individual drawings take their place as exemplars of the necessary mastery of drawing that precedes an approach to colour rendering. The majority of his drawings are usually conceived as independent works not as studies for paintings. They are studies from the living model, intended to keep Matisse in touch with direct observation. They treat the human form in isolation, almost as if it were being studied as a sculpture, before integration as one element of a greater pictorial scheme (where the structural drawing is conceived as a function of the painting process). Indeed, small *académies*, rendered in rather naturalistic foreshortening, are to be found inserted into the paintings as images of Matisse's own sculpture. Thus the drawings mediate between

23. Russell, *Meanings*, vol. 1, p. 40.

Matisse *Dance (First Version)*
(early 1909). Oil on canvas
2597 × 3901 mm

the two-dimensional and three-dimensional and the real and artistic on more than one level. The drawings, incorporated as separate figurative motifs into the paintings, can be seen as the point of contact between the synthetic preconception of the painting structure and the naturalistic observation of form, so that form in the paintings and drawings always moves both towards and away from reality.

But the drawings are continuous with the paintings in other ways: first, as black on white, they represent studies in value contrast. In his painting, initially, Matisse translates contrast in value to contrast in colour. In a drawing method that interchanges negative and positive areas, Matisse substitutes colour contrast for exposed line and lets the contrast do the drawing. Thus he effectively renders volume, while maintaining the flat spatial advantage of the drawing mode, and creates light as the function of the colour ground (as light is the function of the drawing sheet). This puts in place one element of the century's new pictorial structure: the picture itself as a source of light.

Matisse also uses black as a colour in painting. Black and white give each other their full value, one as light, the other as the essence of colour, as Matisse repeatedly explained later about his drawings. In his paintings from 1914 on, the introduction of black as colour rendered a more profound system of colour contrasts and analogies than the system which used black only for line. Black became the key in the same painting for both value and colour contrasts.

Dance shows how the drawing system worked to create the first truly nonperspectival space in twentieth-century art. The dancers are rendered as individual, self-enclosed contours; the subject becomes the pretext for linking them. The linking is done by conceiving of the arms as connected by a series of opposed contour lines, attached to one another in a chain of long ovoids, opening into one another and severely flattened by their radically simplified contours. The figures and ground are given as colour contrasts emphasised by black outline drawing. The structure is rendered by the drawing as a system of contrasted positives (figures) and negatives (areas between) on the same plane. In *Dance* the saturated

Matisse *The Moroccans* (1916). Oil on canvas. 1813 × 2794 mm

blue of the sky and green of the grass are so close (and they are also close on the spectrum) that they maintain themselves on the same plane.

This system yields in some subsequent pictures to a ground expressed as one colour. In *The Red Studio* (1911),[24] the emphasis shifts; the unform, continuous red ground is rendered as a positive and becomes a means of drawing. The flood of colour embracing everything stops only for the underground line, which it leaves as if protected by dikes. It passes through the delineated objects and around other more solid, locally coloured ones, to create a complex counterpoint of negative and positive objects and spaces, all rendered now as positive.

This method of drawing did not render a complete or flexible enough system to constitute a new pictorial structure. As a tool, however, it enabled Matisse to integrate to his pictorial means the new Cubist structural inventions that Picasso had begun to develop in 1909. Matisse's large decorative painting, *The Moroccans* (1916), [25] reveals the system being employed with great sophistication as various facets of it are by turns isolated and then integrated to a combined construction. The picture, in its juxtaposition of organic and architectural elements shows clearly Matisse's incorporation of synthetic and constructive modes and how they are integrated with his drawing. In the positive areas the figures are defined, as in the individual drawings, by contour drawing. As the forms drawn in contour pass over into space, the method of delineating them changes. They are now given as the product of the enveloping black ground. The pot held by the Arab shows this most clearly. The independent black contour lines are withdrawn to the ground which now establishes the perimeters of the forms; it flows between gourds and leaves where it is too thick to be read as line except in one small area where the positive plane is reasserted in pink, and the drawing is again given as contour.

As a result, form is the product of the interchange of positive and negative areas; this renders the contour plastically and expressively continuous with colour. Thus two conflicts with ordinary vision are set in motion, and a major theme is made apparent by the drawing: the

24. The Museum of Modern Art, New York. Mrs Simon Guggenheim Fund.

25. The Museum of Modern Art, New York. Gift of Mr and Mrs Samuel A. Marx.

relocation of the real in the constructed. It is this that becomes the driving force of the late cut-paper works.

There can be little doubt that at this point Matisse had been looking carefully at the Cubist collage, particularly the more complex examples.[26] He had integrated the constructive approach with his own synthetic approach and accepted a new structure as the organising principle of the work (discussed in detail in connection with Picasso and Braque since it is their invention), one implied by Matisse's own drawing system of form organised by an implicit overall linear armature parallel to the picture plane and aligned in conformity with the rectangular format of the painting, creating a planar division of space. The juxtaposition of the real with the constructed is given in *The Moroccans*, as in certain other paintings, by the depiction of three motifs studied as separate drawings from different points of view, now organised according to a unified conception. The dislocation of ordinary vision – spatial disjunction and changes of scale – seems clearly to have been suggested by the relationship of collage elements to ground in the work of Picasso and Braque, but integrated into Matisse's more synthetic (and stable) view of the world. Matisse was then free to work the two systems in concert, asserting one over the other as he chose, as the dominant expressive means.

There is one more important feature of *The Moroccans* (as an exemplar) to be discussed. The unifying ground is black; thus the ground is no longer a source of reflected light, rather, it absorbs light, as if the canvas were a whole world and not just the staging ground for forms. In *The Moroccans* one sees the architectonic forms and the figures and still lifes operating in concert, integrated by the basic notion of drawing. It is also possible to imagine them freed from one another: the effect of their sharp silhouetting against the very ground that holds them, as happens in the late *papiers collés*, for example *Memory of Oceania* (1953),[27] where coloured forms liberated from their enveloping ground are combined in a different and far freer more complex manner. Matisse wrote:

> 'The paper cut-out enables me to draw in colour. For me this represents a simplification. Instead of drawing the contour and installing the colour within it – each modifying the other – I draw directly in colour, which is all the more measured since it is not transposed. This simplification guarantees precision in the uniting of the two mediums, which now make one. . . . Cutting into the raw colour reminds me of the direct carving of the sculptors. . . . Scissors can acquire more feeling for line than pencil or charcoal'.[28]

The effect of radically simplified contour drawing, seen in the drawings of the 1930s and '40s, but more apparent in the paintings in which the ground silhouettes them, had all along been the rendering of form as flat and on the same plane with the ground:

> 'Flat, unmodulated areas read as pattern . . . we see the shape of the area and are conscious of its silhouette. . . . As the sense of space and form disappear, the decorative pattern becomes more evident, one's attention concentrates on shape relationships rather than on seeing the three dimensional complexities.'[29]

Cutting withdrew the drawn line so that contour was plastically coextensive with colour but liberated from the enveloping ground. At

26. For example, *Bowl with Fruit, Violin, and Wine Glass*, 1912. Philadelphia Museum of Art. A. E. Gallatin Collection. Daix 530. Z.II**385.

27. The Museum of Modern Art, New York. Mrs Simon Guggenheim Fund.

28. Henri Matisse, quoted in Pierre Schneider, *Henri Matisse: Exposition Centenaire* (Paris: Grand Palais, 1970), p. 48.

29. Daniel M. Mendelowitz, *Drawing* (Stanford, Calif.: Stanford University Press, 1967), p. 326.

the same time, all the power that had been accruing to contour drawing, was realised in the cutting.

The relocation of the real in the constructed, which had created unexpected changes from ordinary vision in the paintings is reinterpreted in the cut-paper works. Liberation of the figure from a uniform ground in order to attach it to a new ground constructed a new kind of optical disjunction in the plane, giving additional power to the edge. Cutting the forms from the ground created a new spatial freedom: the ground and figures could engage in spatial relationships only implied in painting. In *The Swimming Pool* (1952),[30] this relocation is the result of the compression of movement to the contours and the release of form into space. The composition moves from figures with simple silhouettes to those with complex silhouettes (and back). The latter are the result of the compression of many movements into one contour: as the movement builds in the contours the figures leap out of ordinary space. The viewer, in the centre of the room, is surrounded by an optical phenomenon, a flat plane twisting in relation to the motion of the figures. The dislocation of the real (the form) in the constructed (the space) becomes the guiding principle of the work.

For Picasso, too, the issue was the survival of three-dimensional form under the new condition of the gradual disappearance of the spatial illusion created by linear perspective. Picasso was trained in the Beaux-Arts tradition and for him the key to a new structure, a new space, lay in the drawing of the figure as a self-contained sculptural object. He had been brought up on the academic linear convention (his father was a drawing master). To an artist like Picasso, whose apprehension of form was tactile and concrete, line, as the only reality, became the structural principle and backbone of the work. Line was the means to feel out the initial structure of form, which was then given the illusion of solidity by the play of light on its surfaces, creating contrast and shadow, expressed by the convention of shading in the form of hatching. Colour was a function of surface, restricted to local forms; it had no immediate structural role and, therefore, in the initial exploration of a new spatial construction, was not of interest.

Picasso began as a contour draughtsman; his Cubist period represents the analytic fracturing and reassembly of the contour of the human figure and the head (and still-life forms related to these by formal analogy) by means of a manipulation of the conventional drawing system. The exploration of a new spatial construction was undertaken as a kind of partnership between Picasso and Braque (who unfortunately left very few drawings), each contributing in turn. Drawing seems to have been for Braque a function of painting: structural drawing took place in the painting process and was buried in or integrated with it, so that while Braque actually produced the first Cubist paintings,[31] Picasso, the draughtsman trained in the academy, took up the intensive linear analysis of form that led to the new pictorial structure, focusing on the vocabulary of drawing itself, to locate the structural principle of the work.

In Cubist drawing the question of the survival of imagery becomes one of internal structure; with no objective perspective the image must establish its own space. The establishment of that space becomes a question of literal scale determined by internal reference; a reason why the figure, head, and still life became the archetypal images (they present surface relationships which can be easily measured). In *The*

30. The Museum of Modern Art, New York. Mrs Bernard F. Gimbel Fund.

31. Braque remained interested more in the relationships among forms than in the analysis of the inner structure of one form and its extension by analogies to relationships among forms (an essential difference also between Matisse and Picasso).

Mill at Horta (1909) (fig. 16) we first see the abolition of objective perspective in the relief modeling of the planes of the buildings, in a stepwise composition. An important peculiarity of this view of Horta is that the town is given as a self-contained form, with the planar articulations of individual buildings as the internal subdivisions of a conceptual whole. Within this self-contained form, the individual buildings are seen from more than one point of view; they are spread to the plane and tilt up off axis to present us with views we would not normally see. The composition is circular, the eye is always led in measured steps back from the surface, where it is stopped and moved sideways and around by the elision of measured plane into measured plane, and back out, a wilful rearrangement of natural appearances.

While *Horta* is not typical for Picasso, since it is a landscape and drawn in colour, it does establish several important points about Cubism. As a landscape it refers not simply to the colours of Horta, but to the colours of the traditional watercolour rendering before Cézanne's fracturing of form; it therefore announces that solid form is again being examined. Thus *Horta* inaugurates the investigation of Cubism in Picasso's work as a threefold study: first, as the analysis of the surfaces of self-contained complex forms and their constructive attachments as expressed by their contours and their internal subdivisions; second, as the uniting of analogous forms in one complex form, the attachment of form to form; and third, as the examination and analysis – the restructuring – of the picture itself as a self-contained complex form, articulated by its internal divisions.

The Mill at Horta also showed Picasso that forms should be analogised according to the place where they reside: the square format of the framing edge and the flat picture plane. Form will thus be treated as architectonic regardless of the subject. The investigation is one of pictorial structure; pictorial unity will depend on the destruction of particularities and peculiarities (personalities) of forms as well as on the creation of analogies (likenesses) among them. Likeness in Cubist drawing exists not only in part-to-part structural likeness but also in visual metaphors between different classes of objects: thus the body is like a violin, the violin suggests how a cheek may be curved, it becomes an ear, extending the analogies even to the sense of hearing. (Personality will be given back to forms by details inserted into the whole, or later by the messages coded into the structure by lettering or collaged newspaper stories.) Furthermore, *The Mill at Horta* makes clear that in the reduced space, and with the disappearance of traditional modeling tied to perspective, it had become necessary, if one was to have a sense of the figure or object as in any way three-dimensional, to grasp it as whole, to present the views of it that were hidden in perspective vision but suggested by the conventions of shading and modeling used in conjunction with perspective. Following *Horta*, Picasso began to study individual forms in intense detail, not just as they are known from ordinary sight but as the artist knows them, not just from disparate views but from a complex of sensations and perceptions as well.

African sculpture had been important to Picasso in studies for *Les Demoiselles d'Avignon* (1907),[32] which had shown the first sign of planar rendering of the figure in his work (although its formal relationships are more like those in Matisse's work). Masks, especially, showed him form that was already studied as a system of planar analogies. In *Head of a Medical Student* (1907) (pl. IV) it is apparent that Picasso's formal

32. The Museum of Modern Art, New York. Acquired through the Lillie P. Bliss Bequest.

apprehension of the planar articulation of African sculpture was linear; line thus became his unit for articulating the planar changes and connections in Cubism, mediating between form conceived as three-dimensional and the expression of it in a flat, two-dimensional medium. Immediately following *Les Demoiselles*, as we can see in the *Sheet of Studies* (1908), Picasso had already begun somewhat schematic studies of the musculature of the human figure and its most expressive part, the face, to re-examine its external structural attachments according to its internal musculature: *Head* (1909) (fig. 16) relates this study to the architectonic forms of *Horta*.

In *Mlle Léonie* (1911–12) (fig. 19), we see how a transition from the 'natural' to the artificial and conceptual, from the contour to the plane, is achieved and how the form is presented to us as virtually whole, in a departure from ordinary vision. The *contrapposto* pose is an especially interesting one in that it represents the body turning in space to present more than one view. Its challenge and opportunity is therefore double; any representation of it is already a conceptualisation of a double view. In *Mlle Léonie* the *contrapposto* of the 1908 *Sheet of Studies* is now expressed as an extraordinary quadruple view: the upper section is given as split from the crown of the head between classically sculptural chiarascuro rendering at the back to planar linear rendering at the front. At the top, despite the split in treatment, the view of the head and shoulders is a unified three-quarter view, given in half-shadow. The two views are attached at the shoulder where they separate into two planes. As it descends, the front plane twists towards a suggestion of full frontality in its lower triangular section. Below the shoulder the back twists into full back view, rendered in shadow; at the buttocks its rendering changes to a linear, flat, planar form emerging abruptly from the shadow to attach tangentially to the frontal upper plane. Both planes are rendered as in full light. Thus a full view of the torso is given as turning within a very shallow space, rendered as a shadow which interchanges with the shadow of the more conventionally rendered shoulder and crown of the head; the figure and its shadows have, in fact, constructed one another.

Two other things about the drawing are important. First, each of the four views is organised as a separate planar area, its details described by linear forms and cross-hatched shadow lines contained within it (although referred to the external shadows); second, inserted into this constructive system are the survivors of a notional reality, the breasts and buttocks, making a point of the purely conceptual nature of the rest, while they add to our sense that we are not dealing with ordinary visual experience. They are to a large extent the condition of the drawing's survival as an image of reality. *Mlle Léonie* is the creature of her own shadows: the interchange of external and internal shadows expressed as a system apart from the linear, planar structure maintains an illusion of space, although radically shallow at this point.

From 1910 on, this intimate knowledge of the figure (and especially the details of the head) had been, increasingly, the knowledge of the picture itself. Cubist analytic drawing was not itself the means by which the artist arrived at a finished concept; rather, the investigation was continued into the painting, where its complexities multiplied and it found its logical culmination. The attachments of the planes of the face and body expressed as a linear armature became the structure and soul of the picture itself, as the linear analysis of planar forms of the head and the body were extended to a linear armature of the whole surface.

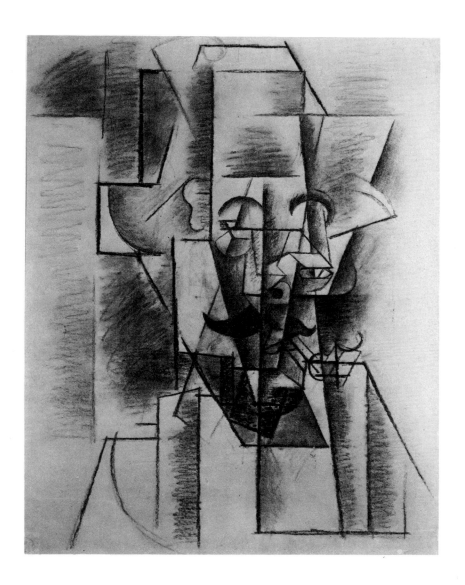

Picasso *Man with Pipe* (1912).
Charcoal. 622 × 470 mm

Thus between 1910 and 1912 another element of the new pictorial
structure, the linear armature, was firmly in place, organising the
surface as a system of shallow planes.

However, it became increasingly difficult for Picasso to insist on the
shallow, illusionary space. The depiction of the object as the creature of
its own shadows and the illusionistic dappling of light as it modulated
volumes in the paintings did nothing to dispel the insistent two-dimen-
sionality of the tactile surface; that and the drawing, the linear scaffolding, constantly reinforced the tautness of the plane. In 1912, in the
drawing *Man with a Pipe*,[33] Picasso reasserted line as line of connection.
The line that had threatened to break down completely into a system of
signs, from time to time, between 1910 and 1912, was now reasserted
as a kind of geometricised enclosure drawing; the line, reasserted, func-
tioned as a line of connection between notional objects and between the
remnants of disparate perspectives, given by shadow. *Man with a Pipe*
insists on itself as almost a relief, reversing its perspectives.

Picasso had, in fact, in 1912 begun to construct in three dimensions,

33. Collection Dr Israel Rosen,
Baltimore.

first a cardboard guitar (analysing an already constructed object as a start) and then, as *Study for a Construction* (1912) (fig. 18) shows, the figure itself (a version of *Mlle Léonie* analysed as the structural relative of the guitar). Now, by concentrating on one element of the conventional drawing system, the linear structure, and dropping for the moment the shadow system, it became possible in the drawings to get rid of the space of illusionism. In 1910 Braque had introduced lettering to the Cubist configuration (another factor mitigating against illusionist space); he now, in 1912, introduced pasted paper in answer to Picasso's pasting oilcloth onto canvas. Both were attempts to assert reality and solidity — to find a space for objects. In the face of the fast disappearing space of shadow illusionism the surface was the last resort.

Picasso inserted Braque's *papier collé* into this linear armature, in effect making the connection between the two-dimensional and the three-dimensional structural rather than simply notative, and making the linear armature the 'home' of objective reality. *Papier collé* also became the means for reintroducing colour. Initially a function of surface, it had no place in the painted structure; but it had a structural function in collage in that it was physically coextensive with the patch of paper; contour delineation was withdrawn to the cut edge, making drawing a function of colour construction as well as line. Colour was therefore a function of collage's assertion of physical reality. The pieces of paper exist as real in themselves, independent of the illusion into which they are incorporated; modified by drawing, shading, and the other means of illusionism, they move both towards and away from reality. Now the unexpected visual element in the structure was real: 'The difference between the collage materials [and the surface] creates the same discontinuity as that which exists between the different planes in real space.'[34] The dislocation of ordinary vision was now a function of construction.

The insertion of pieces of paper into the Cubist scaffolding changed the basis of pictorial illusionism. The pictorial view was no longer intact; the multiple viewpoints, rendered as if from a single pictorial viewpoint in earlier work, became more selective, and the planar disjunction became a new structural means in which disjunctive elements were joined to the illusion of a seamless whole. Line became a connective between the collage elements and the surface of the picture itself, as the elements of collage slid under and over one another. Elements of representation were made to coexist with constructed elements. The careful examination of each object as a whole gave way to partial representation of more broadly drawn forms. Scale was no longer a function of notional reality, but of the construction itself; it was part-to-part, relative scale, referred to an overall non-hierarchical arrangement of elements. Images were made up of pieces of themselves that may have had any kind of physical identity: it became possible to introduce all sorts of non-art materials, to incorporate entire ready-made images from reproductions, textures from wallpaper, and newspapers, which served as the optical texture that hatching had previously served and as the means to identify the subject through the narrative, giving back personality.

With collage reality is dismantled and reconstructed at will; the variable viewpoint allows a kind of selective roving through the picture, almost as though one were inside it. The means has become the motif, and the motif and means project their linear structures as the structure

34. Pierre Daix, *Le Cubisme de Picasso* (Neuchatel: Editions Ides et Calendes, 1979), pp. 103–128.

Picasso *Painter and Model* 1928.
Oil on canvas. 1499 × 2312 mm

35. The Museum of Modern Art, New
York. The Sidney and Harriet Janis
Collection (fractional gift).

of twentieth-century art, putting in place the new pictorial structure that
replaces perspective.

Now the Cubist picture, too, became its own source of light and the
coloured papers became their own light source; they were no longer
dependent on the illusionism of reflected light.

Collage was an inspired reinterpretation of the conventional drawing
system: each element − colour, contour, shading, texture − could
operate as an independent element or, indeed, as an independent
aesthetic system. The linear element, thus isolated, could move towards
analysis and the armature broken apart, or it could be used synthetically
to find figures (as in the work of Klee and Joan Miró) in conjunction with
the basic planar structure it had engendered in the first place, or
asserted in conjunction with the planes as abstractions, as in the work of
Mondrian. Or, as *The Moroccans* showed, the basic structure could
accept representational elements and was open also to metaphoric
allusion and symbolic reference. Line could also find abstract organic
forms, as in Jean Arp's work, and accommodate as well to impersonal
handling as to the most expressive gesturing. The colour plane could be
left to stand alone. The result is a continuous discourse, in twentieth-
century art among abstract and representational, organic and geometric forms.

Picasso was now free to elaborate his own invention, sometimes even
seeming to drop it. Yet if he is seen as basically a contour draughtsman,
in the convention of the academy, whose Cubist phase is an analytic
fracturing and reassembly of enclosure drawing, one sees the possi-
bility of discussing the seeming discontinuities and contradictions of his
later work in a different light. If we follow him from *Man in a Melon Hat*
(1914) (fig. 21), to *Ricciotto Canudo* (1918) and *Nessus and Dejanira*
(1920) (fig. 22), we see him gradually reasserting classical drawing,
finally, in works like *Sleeping Peasants* (1919), emerging to full volumetric
rendering, but now subject to the Cubist experiment. Perhaps it is this
seeming paradox he pictured in *Painter and Model* (1928),[35] in which

the Cubist painter contemplates a geometricised bust which he is busy drawing as a naturalistic profile on the canvas in his studio.[36]

As the new century focused on the new structure of line and colour plane as elements to be manipulated, both structurally and as physical realities, a number of possibilities presented themselves almost immediately. It is no accident that the work central to the Futurists' idea of simultaneity — the concept that 'a picture must be a synthesis of what is remembered and what has been seen, a synthetic visual impression comprising not merely the various aspects of a single object, but any feature related to it, physically or psychologically'[37] — namely Umberto Boccioni's series *States of Mind* (1911) (fig. 37), is tied to a train journey. The Boccioni series consists of three preliminary, though finished, drawings in charcoal, three paintings and three smaller pen-and-ink drawings after the paintings. There is an interesting difference between the two sets of drawings — almost a lesson in what drawing can achieve as a medium for thinking. The pencil drawings reflect the indirect influence of Cubism, while the paintings and subsequent drawings reflect the direct influence of Cubism. The feeling of search, almost an awkwardness, in the charcoal studies is in total contrast to the mechanically assured summation of the pen-and-ink drawings.

Simultaneity was rendered plastically by a shift from the *passage* of Cubism to the interpenetration of planes and volumes by means of discontinuous contours that interlocked. Boccioni himself gave the power of expression to the line:

'We have declared in our manifesto that what must be rendered is the dynamic *sensation* . . . the particular rhythm of each object, its inclination, its movement, or, to put it more exactly, its interior forces. . . . What is overlooked is that all inanimate objects display by their lines, calmness or frenzy, sadness or gaiety. These various tendencies lend to the lines of which they are formed a sense of character of weighty stability or aerial lightness. Every object reveals by its lines how it would resolve itself were it to follow the tendencies of its forces. This decomposition is not governed by fixed laws but it varies according to the characteristic personality of the object and emotions of the onlooker.'[38]

But we are dealing now with drawing styles themselves which represent a selection and elaboration of what was won earlier, so that while these statements are revolutionary, we now have a developing tradition.

Simultaneity of physical forces, expressed by repetition of linear accents (as well as interaction of colour) was also an important idea for Robert Delaunay, as in *The Tower and the Wheel* (1910). For Fernand Léger, as we can see in *Verdun, the Trench Diggers* (1916) (fig. 29), it meant the simultaneous presence of the three pictorial elements of line, form and colour, all used in a system of deliberate contrasts. In Léger's later figurative work these contrasts were retained but organised by radical contour drawing to monumental effect. Léger and Delaunay were among the first to move away from pure Cubism into abstraction. Marcel Duchamp, however, took the idea of the mechanical more literally and was not interested in abstraction, noting later that he had wished to put art once again at the service of the mind when he began to look, between 1910 and 1912, for 'an absolutely concise co-ordinate drawing with no relation to arty handwork.'[39] He thus delivered a key

36. In the middle of the nineteenth century Charles Baudelaire had called for 'the painter of modern life', describing him in 1845 as the artist whose art would 'create a suggestive magic containing both the object and the subject, the world exterior to the artist and the artist himself'. (Quoted in Joseph C. Sloane, *French Painting between the Past and the Present*, Princeton, N.J.: Princeton University Press, 1951, pp. 81–2.) Sloane notes about Baudelaire: 'The object of his search was a figure painter, for though the landscape was certainly one of the fields in which the art of the future was being prepared, man's fate in society was of the greatest concern to thinking people of the day, and what was needed above all were the painters to set him down, noble or not, against the background of the life he was going to have to live, apparently deprived of the solace of orthodox religion and the inspiration of the classical ages'. If Picasso's collage creatures are modern men, he still continues to muse on the classical ages, after first offering the primitive as a possible replacement for orthodox religion.

37. John Golding, *Cubism: A History and Analysis* (London: Faber and Faber, 1959), p. 43.

38. Boccioni, quoted in Max Kozloff, *Cubism/Futurism* (New York: Harper & Row, 1973), pp. 161–2.

39. Russell, *Meanings*, vol. 6, p. 16.

idea to the constructors of the 1920s: the depersonalisation or the elimination of the hand already implicit in Cubism itself. From one place to another in the second decade of the century, the notion was the artist-constructor. Drawing in Germany, The Netherlands and Russia, following from Cubism, gradually conformed, via the mechanical, to the ideal of the abstract. Cubism, not an abstract style itself, gave birth, through the technique of collage more than anything else, to abstraction and to the notion of painting and sculpture as constructions. Mondrian believed that Cubism had never followed through fully its implications and was convinced that line detached from figuration would produce more spiritual forms. He was convinced of the ethical nature of abstraction as 'indicative of the spiritual evolution of modern culture'.[40]

Robert Welsh points out that the Museum of Modern Art's drawing, *Church Facade* (1914) (fig. 45), is one of several skeletal line drawings 'which were then or later reinforced with India ink or gouache'.[41] *Church Facade* represents the stage before ink or gouache additions but, nevertheless, the thickening of parts of the lines to the point where they are more like planar objects than lines gives ample evidence of Mondrian's assignment of an increasingly objective character to the linear structure.[42]

In Mondrian's drawing, line represents the structural principle of the work. 'In order to express in form the power that emanates from nature, lines must generally be made much blacker in the plastic arts than one sees them in nature.'[43] To line, particularly vertical line, and to black Mondrian accorded the primary structural function: line was male, black was male, and colour as well as horizontal and curved elements provided harmony. The spiritual essence of form was associated with masculine verticals, the material essence with 'recumbent' female, horizontal form. According to Welsh, Mondrian's probable method was to work back and forth between painting and drawing: as the painting developed so the drawing developed. Drawing was probably used as the means for maintaining the dominance of the structural male elements over the colouristic female elements, harmonising them and keeping them in order. The black lines 'spontaneously produce' the passive rectangular colour planes, and the drawing, therefore, to Mondrian probably became an essentially masculine expression and, one can infer, more spiritual than painting.

Church Facade and its associated drawings represent a unique moment in Mondrian's work in which he worked persistently with the notion of objective line, evolved from the identification of line with planar objects in his 'plus-minus' drawings, so that his line always 'remembered' it was once an object. This drawing, in fact, illustrates just how his line became 'objective'.

In Russia abstract art developed from 1912 on, after initial contact with Cubism and Futurism, out of a search for new values and new solutions, a search for the spiritual art. Manipulating the basic elements of colour plane, the line of direction, and the picture plane as an infinite abstract space that implied universality, the Russians presented a new idea of reality. The real consisted in the intrinsic elements of art — the materials, colours, the lines and the basic forms. These, manipulated as concrete elements in both two and three dimensions, took the artist into the non-objective world. From 1914 on, especially following the Revolution in 1917, and into the mid-1920s the artist-engineer con-

40. Robert Welsh, quoted in 'Mondrian as Draftsman', in *Mondrian* (Stuttgart: Staatsgalerie, 1980), p. 49.

41. Ibid.

42. Ibid. The Museum's drawing is related to *Composition 1916*, The Solomon R. Guggenheim Museum, New York, and to a second painting in Kyoto, *Composition 1916 in Black and White*.

43. Ibid.

tinued to construe the non-objective as the basic elements of a new reality, indeed of a new social order.

In northern Europe the conceptual principle was given primacy and elevated to the spiritual, which recalls Seurat's notions of the golden section and the spiritual nature of his linear system, and the Neoplatonic conceptions of form and matter that Kandinsky, too, was involved with in Germany by the end of the first decade of the century.

In Germany and Austria a series of Expressionist styles emerged in different centres following Jugendstil and the Secession movements. Among these styles were *Die Brücke* in Dresden and *Der Blaue Reiter* in Munich. Differing from Fauvism in its angularity and a nervous fragmentation that imparts to both the synthetic line and formal structure of the drawing a kind of psychic restlessness and nervous drive, Expressionism, like its counterpart in France, is a style in which each plastic element – line, form, colour, light and space – has been made pictorially largely self-sufficient. In the Kirchner drawing *Street Scene, Berlin* (1914) (fig. 58), a late example of the style, we can see how line was employed in a hard angular manner, again a change owed to the direct intervention of popular woodcuts and primitive art; indeed, woodcut was the primary graphic means of Expressionism. Here the structure and the linear quality are also influenced by the radical contour drawing of Matisse's nude figures of 1907 in such paintings as *Le Luxe, II*[44] and modified by the angular and more solidly planar definition of Picasso's *Les Demoiselles d'Avignon.*

By the second decade of the century, too, another force was apparent in German art – the symbolic. In the work of Franz Marc it was married to the restless dynamic energy of Futurism. As Werner Haftmann notes in describing Marc: 'The symbols are not accidental . . . the animals . . . link the abstract organism of the picture to poetic experience that had its origin in nature.'[45] As Marc put it himself, 'A symbol arises from a fortuitous impulse'.[46] But his line is different, lighter, more decorative; it derives its quality from yet another source of German art, Jugendstil, which had carried within its decorative arabesque style the seeds of abstraction, but especially of the independent, radical (decorative) contour line. This line, the autographic, had been in use since the beginning of the century; it is basically Gauguin's synthetic line. It can be seen in Egon Schiele's drawing *Woman Wrapped in a Blanket* (1911) (pl. v) and in Oskar Kokoschka's *Nude with Back* (c. 1907) (fig. 56). One of its sources in Germany, too, is ultimately to be found in the German medieval woodcut and the popular contemporary woodcut from which it was adapted by Jugendstil artists.

Kandinsky, a Russian working in Germany and a colleague of Marc in *Der Blaue Reiter*, was a primary practitioner of this line, which can be described as generated both by the vitality of the moving hand and its own vitality, interacting as a kind of physically and emotionally impelled reality. Initially a line of emotional force (though decorative), it goes beyond the idea of drawing as touch in that it has a tendency to abstraction and generalisation as it 'cools' (as it does in Kandinsky's later work, under the influence of Cubism and his more conceptual Russian colleagues). It is usually found either in conjunction with, or in counterpoint to, colour functioning as an autonomous pictorial element but is just as important where colour is used as an evocative surface or pulsating form. In 1910 Kandinsky arrived at an independent abstract mode under the influence of this experimental atmosphere in Germany,

44. Statens Museum for Kunst, Copenhagen. J. Rump Collection.

45. Quoted in Werner Haftmann, *German Art of the Twentieth Century* (New York: The Museum of Modern Art, 1957), p. 18.

46. Ibid.

which was sympathetic to his native Russian spirituality, with its drive to abstract modes of thought, as well as the Neoplatonic and Symbolist ideas of colour as being analogous to the abstractly expressive qualities of music. Initially he built on the energy of the vitalistic line, under the influence also of Fauvism and Matisse. By 1912 he had incorporated Cubist pictorial organisation to his independent abstraction, but he was conceptually, if not structurally, even more dependent on the late landscapes of Cézanne.

Kandinsky came to see line as wholly independent of representation and even of specific form, and infinitely extensible in space. Colour, released from specific material form, although not from objects, was synthetically united to sound as one sensation. It became symbolic of the spiritual, each colour sounded a characteristic note, while the line running freely released the 'pure inner sound' of objects and led towards salvation and resurrection. Weaving line and colour together in an abstract arabesque, Kandinsky advanced the graphological line as a major expressive and structural vehicle capable of synthesising a number of sensations, the auditory as well as the tactile and kinesthetic. For Kandinsky 'the abandonment of natural appearances no longer meant that the artist despised or violated creation; . . . it had become necessary to bring the new and broader conception to the universe to artistic vision'.[47] But this vision corresponded to the artist's own vision of 'the underlying mystical design of the visible world'. Kandinsky wrote:

'A perfect drawing is one where nothing can be changed without destroying the essential inner life, quite irrespective of whether the drawing contradicts our conception of anatomy, botany, or other sciences. The question, is not whether the coincidental outer form is violated but only if its quality depends on the artist's need of certain form irrespective of reality.'[48]

Kandinsky's vision of the universe is essentially Cézanne's landscape turned inwards to the soul and outwards to the universe, its scale expanded by fantasy and its colour and objects released to function as if in a psychic space. Kandinsky contributes this note of spirituality to the line; he conceives of line as abstract, yet organic, metaphoric. The movement of line is equated with the concept of growth — the growth of form and of the spirit. This was a concept of line that Klee and Kandinsky shared, although Klee was not at all interested in pure abstraction. However, Kandinsky's formal emphasis shifted in the 1920s in response to the concept of the artist-engineer prevalent in his homeland. By ceasing to treat the line as an organic connective and taking up instead its function as a line of direction, he achieved a *rapprochement* with objectivity, with the 'reality' of forms in space expressed as geometric abstraction by his Russian colleagues.

Another aspect of German art, the illustrational, was initially expressed by Marc as the aspiration to engage the plastic with the poetic and metaphoric, but with an extra-plastic message. Under the pressure of the First World War it was expressed as the construction of a new realism and the dramatisation of the self. At this point the shadows of Duchamp and Francis Picabia became tangible: ideas of the artist as engineer, fate as mechanistically determined, man as machine, and the artist as constructor of an absurd new reality out of bits and pieces of the old, the Readymade altered, came to the fore in Germany where the Dada movement (christened in 1916 in Switzerland) found its ultimate

47. Ibid., p. 78.
48. Wassily Kandinsky, *On the Spiritual in Art*, ed. Hilla Rebay (New York, 1959), p. 161.

expression. A movement of protest in the midst of war, Dada manifested itself in a deluge of small pieces of paper expressing its disgust. It contributed not a style but an attitude towards making: art was beyond aesthetic consideration, therefore it was open to the incorporation of materials, devices, nonsense attitudes, and irrationalities previously outside art. By the end of the first decade of the century, the Expressionist line, which was tied to representation, became in George Grosz's hands a brittle and mechanical tool of social commentary. By 1920 Grosz depicts his collaborator in the theatre, John Heartfield, as *The Engineer Heartfield* (pl. x):

> 'In agreement with George Grosz, John Heartfield, Johannes Baader, and Hannah Hoch, we decided to call these works photomontages. This term translates our aversion at playing the artists, and thinking of ourselves as engineers we intended to assemble, construct [*montieren*] our works.'[49]

Between 1915 and 1920, while Jean Arp in Switzerland developed automatic drawing, Kurt Schwitters and Max Ernst in Germany developed new aesthetics of collage. Ernst contributed a number of automatic drawing techniques as well, among them *frottage*, or rubbing to induce hallucinatory images from a rough surface placed beneath the drawing sheet. Of these techniques, automatic drawing and collage were the most important. Under the aegis of Freudian free association, automatic drawing provided a kind of direct access to the images of the unconscious and a new subject and new reality – a new psychic reality – were introduced. Used from 1922 on in Paris as one of the mainsprings of Surrealism, automatism was eventually transformed into a pure plastic device and later became the means to a new pictorial strategy in New York for yet another generation of artists. More immediately, a more controlled version of it became the basis for Klee's drawing style, and it is the common pictorial conception that links Klee to Miró.

Arp had initially let chance into his art in his collages of 1915–16, letting the pieces of torn or cut paper fall to the floor and then arranging them on sheets of paper more or less as they had fallen. In 1916 Arp, under the influence of vitalistic line, converted Expressionistic drawing by combining elementary academic notions of drawing with downright doodling into automatic drawing and the beginnings of plastic automatism. Automatic drawing grew out of a kind of determinism, or chance – the deliberate release of the hand from conscious control so that its motion took over without the intercession of a preconceived subject. The hand traced extended convoluted lines which doubled back on themselves to create enclosures or configurations, both negative (or spatial) and positive (or objective). These configurations, which intimated all sorts of life forms, provoked poetic associations, and those which 'expressed his intentions' Arp then filled in. The unaccented or erased linear connections constituted an 'esoteric or mystical bond'.[50] (In Klee's and Miró's drawing, on the other hand, the visible linear connections left constitute a mystical bond.) The flat, biomorphic form abstracted from nature, which became the common iconographic element in Surrealism (as well as Arp's characteristic form) had a peculiar existential quality. Its exaggerated contours rendered it quite flat, making it appear on the same plane – embedded – in its ambient space.

The paradoxical characteristic of this kind of drawing gives rise to

49. Raoul Haussman in 'Courrier Dada', quoted in Dawn Ades, *Dada and Surrealism Reviewed* (London: Arts Council of Great Britain, 1979), 4.29, p. 93.

50. Philip Rawson, *Drawing* (London: Oxford University Press, 1969) p. 141.

Arp's reliefs and provides the connection between the two-dimensional and the three-dimensional in his work. If the connective line between forms is broken, the isolated form, because of its strongly exaggerated contour engraves its drastically flattened form as a contrast to the ground in which it is embedded and exerts pressure against the surface: it is no longer perceived as flat, but as tending to the sculptural. It is a natural step to cut this shape out and to give it a three dimensional identity.

Although the cursive calligraphic definition of enclosures implied in the automatic line is the line that can be traced all the way back to Gothic art, and from there into Art Nouveau and to Gauguin and Matisse in France, to Jugendstil, and Kandinsky in Germany, Arp's use of cursive automatic line as a device to produce formal enclosures takes place in the context of Cubist linear network, giving it new legitimacy.

In 1920 Arp and Ernst, working together in Cologne, began to emphasise the facility of collage for juxtaposing unrelated elements, claiming that the collage process was the 'cultivation of the effects of a systematic displacement'[51] and not dependent on glue. Ernst's collage aesthetic extended beyond collage as such to images in which the juxtaposition of unrelated elements became the principle, whatever the medium. This principle was to produce a miraculous and liberating conciliation of the real and the 'marvelous'. The marvelous could not be apprehended by reason (this was the basis for the idea of the artist as medium or everyman as an artist); it was a function beyond the fantastic, an almost filmic shift in the seamless fabric of reality, to oppose one reality to another, as in Ernst's *Here Everything Is Still Floating* (fig.71) of 1920 (in which the title is by Arp). Taken beyond the photographic and illustrational into painting itself, the principle of the juxtaposition of images provoked by collage provided a principal source of Surrealist iconography. For Ernst, the collage principle was the cultivation of the effects of a systematic displacement.

In 1922 Ernst transferred his inventive genius to Paris where the technical innovations of the Dada years were allied to new poetic attitudes and Freudian analytic theory. Automatic drawing, joined with automatic writing, opened up the inner world of man, the unconscious, for exploration and provided an iconography for its expression.

But in the meantime, in Germany, Klee, one of the great graphic innovators of the century, was emerging. By 1925, working as a teacher in the Bauhaus, he had fully developed the ideas evolved since he had shown as a colleague of Kandinsky in *Der Blaue Reiter*. Working parallel to Kandinsky and Arp, from sources in Jugendstil, Klee had begun to use the mobile contour line even before Arp, although he did not use it as a device with which to invent a vocabulary of forms. Klee represents an interesting phenomenon: an analytical mind applied to a synthetic method. He concentrated on the line itself, on 'the logic of the connective and its implications'.[52] Giving the line a wiry objectivity achieved first in his lithography and etching techniques, Klee deployed it as if he were a medium, in control but controlled. One important thing about his line is that images are seemingly found by it, as it were, along the way: 'An active line on a walk, moving freely, without a goal. A walk for a walk's sake. The same line accompanied by complementary forms. The same circumscribing itself',[53] and on until he had discovered in the moving line the images and structures of his fantasy. With Klee we constantly re-experience the process of formation of the work, as we

51. Louis Aragon, 'Challenge to Painting' (1930), quoted in Lucy Lippard, *Surrealists on Art* (Englewood Cliffs, N.J.: Prentice-Hall, 1969), p. 39.

52. Rawson, *Drawing*, p. 141.

53. Paul Klee, *Pedagogical Sketchbook* (New York: Frederick A. Praeger, 1959), part 1 (1925).

did with Seurat, but in a linear mode. Klee's line also, along the way, accommodates itself to collage forms; he also exploits the patch of paint as an expressive device.

Another important point about Klee's line is that, as a line that retraces itself, it tends to create nets or grids; these are easily aligned with the Cubist grid and can form a secure conceptual net for the patch of paint which in a few works is liberated to construct an overall image. Line and colour are plastically independent; line takes over as the means to elicit form from a passive, complementary ground of colour or to order its placement. The means for creating line is continuous from one medium to another, the sharp tool that effects the transfer drawing in *The Angler* (1921) also traces a kind of sgraffito into the ground of oil and gouache works on canvas and others. This technique, of drawing indirectly through tracing and transfer, accrues accidental nuance to the line; touch is rendered as the product of accident, and is distanced. Thus another important modern conception, the cooling of touch in drawing (one inherent in Picasso's Cubist rendering and in the substitution of collage elements for hand rendering), is incorporated into his art. It is also a synthesis of those two conceptions of twentieth-century art, the analytic and synthetic, in that it incorporates the Analytic Cubist grid and the collage with the line of radical contour. It incorporates the closely interwoven ground of Cubism and its sense of the painting as an object lit artificially from within to render a new imaginary atmosphere that is not the product of observation. Often it is deliberately detached from the world by Klee's pasting the drawing sheet to a mount and carefully naming it.

Joan Miró, too, was a consummate draughtsman-painter working with a synthesis of collage forms (indeed a number of his paintings are studied from collages, one from machine illustrations, their outlines synthesised to biomorphic forms) and an automatic wiry line. Miró comes from another tradition, but the ubiquity of this line transcends the separate strands of modernism and by the 1920s forms a common plastic heritage. Miró stands at the juncture of Cubist and Surrealist modes, his collage-like forms and meandering lines form themselves into an explicit, though broken, Cubist grid at times, while on other occasions they scrawl and turn into writing and then back into an image and levitate between the organic and the geometric. While Miró is a more monumental painter than Klee, both artists nevertheless have in common this basic conception of wiry kinetic lines exploring the frontal plane, meeting and exploring creatures of their abundant fantasies while a subtly modulated plane of ambient colour and light backlights the drama.

The late 1920s and '30s were years in which the tradition of modernism took firm hold. Artists had consolidated the years of experiment and frequently produced astonishingly beautiful works within the new conventions as well as assimilating their discoveries to more conservative, seemingly retardataire works, which are subtly altered, since nothing remained unaffected by the formal innovations of the first two decades. The majority of drawings in the first part of the twentieth century, like those of Matisse, are conceived within the mode of the mastery of drawing that precedes an approach to colour rendering, even when they are conceived as fully independent or are themselves coloured. They are, however, no longer subject to the rules of linear perspective. Even in works which seem to return to an academic figurative style, the new spatial conditions following from Cubism must now always be considered. Juan Gris's *Max Jacob* (1919) and Picasso's *Ricciotto Canudo* are but two examples of this application of new to old.

The Second World War temporarily disrupted this extraordinarily rich and creative fabric of European art, sending some artists to temporary exile in America and isolating others. Following the war in Europe Jean Dubuffet emerged as a new exponent of automatic drawing now allied to the childish and primitive, to street scrawls and the urban scene as well as the countryside.

Drawing had long been in disrepute in the United States. It was neither a means for analysis (preliminary drawing was 'Renaissance') nor a laboratory for ideas, nor was it an independent mode. With the transferral of the Surrealists, in particular Max Ernst, Stanley William Hayter, André Masson and Matta to New York in 1939 and 1941, it began to appear that automatic drawing was a legitimate and progressive means of working, the initial impulse being that it provided access to a universal, though individual, vocabulary of forms drawn from the unconscious for artists in search of an image. Identifying his private myth with the universal, himself with the mythic, the artist became his own subject, and through the intercession of Freud and Jung, the individual psyche became the model for a world view.

In the winter of 1947, in New York, Jackson Pollock created a new synthesis of the pictorial elements of colour and line. For Pollock, long a disciple of Picasso, the problem was one of finding a way round Picasso to a means for picture-making distinctly his own. The stakes were very high, in that he and his colleagues felt that no American had yet succeeded in joining the mainstream of European art, or in developing out of American art, a form of advanced art that could stand with the most progressive European styles.

Pollock, looking for a way to objectify, to transform the personal and mythical to a universal view, took up automatic drawing. Uniting a technical innovation of Ernst's (dripping paint from a can suspended on a string) with previous experiments of his own in dripping and spattering, he put drawing and painting together; that is, he synthesised colour to linear rendering, integrating contour drawing with colour sensations. Pollock rolled the canvas out flat on the floor and began to pour and spatter enamel house paint onto the canvas, directing the flow of paint with a stick or the handle of a brush, into a line that moved over the ground in response to the movement of his wrist and body and constantly redoubled over itself to build a field of equally accented and distributed elements, created by the constant intersection of line.

> 'There has never been enough said about Jackson Pollock's draftsmanship, that amazing ability to quicken a line by thinning it, to slow it by flooding, to elaborate that simplest of means, the line — to change, to reinvigorate, to extend, to build up an embarrassment of riches in the mass by drawing alone. And each change in the individual line is what every draftsman has always dreamed of, colour'.[54]

Moving off the easel onto the floor was the final step in the destruction of painting as an image of the world, of the canvas itself as a pictorial object. The canvas was now literally the 'ground', and as such its space became wholly non-specific; scale was strictly a function of internal part-to-part relationships. Cézanne's landscape was re-created, but it

54. Frank O'Hara, *Jackson Pollock* (New York: George Braziller, 1959). p. 26.

was not simply painted parallel with nature; the painting became a literal extension of the artist's vitality, of his life force: 'I am nature'.[55] The painting, re-created as the arena of personal experience, also represented the arena of ethical decisions; as extensions of life decisions, painting decisions became ethical ones.[56] Painting became 'the experience of our age in terms/of painting – not an illustration of –/(but the equivalent)/Concentrated/fluid'.[57]

Automatic drawing freed Pollock from Picasso, but it is a technique, not a style. Now, going behind Picasso, Pollock put himself in the place where Picasso began, confronting the work of Cézanne, Seurat, Gauguin and (initially) van Gogh, even going behind them to Impressionism. Pollock based his art on the sensations of light given by colour and reflection but, as a pragmatic American, on light not only from the interaction of colour and the reserve areas of ground but on light as given by direct reflection from the use of reflective materials – bits of glass mirrors and shiny objects incorporated into the surface of the work, and aluminium paint. There are, moreover, all the intervening inventions, the Cubist grid that provides a kind of infrastructure for the works, and the automatic synthetic line that loops back and forth over itself cleaving to this infrastructure. His paintings (and a series of drawings from 1944–7) suggest that Pollock took up the very issues Cézanne had faced so anxiously. In effect, this linear tracing synthesises Cézanne's contour marks and shadow paths with his pattern of colour modulations, and because it is only the trace of its own process, wholly non-objective, it describes neither objects nor the edges of planes. It is literally its own object, all the light and shadow and drawing and painting are absorbed into it. In the great works of 1950–51, what had once been a black contour line in Pollock's work is integrated with the new configuration, interacting with the lines of colour and those of reflection, and is also wholly non-objective. The effect of his field is to dissolve the material substance of the paintings into a field of light, without giving up the specificity of its elements.

Having thus, in a sense, recapitulated the notion that 'as one paints one draws', Pollock addressed himself to the problem of contour drawing as such and the problem of reconciling figuration to sensation and to the field. He had already attempted this in painting, although not successfully, since figuration to Pollock seems to have been a function of drawing; thus the integration of contour drawing, black line, to painting is in a sense a logical next step (challenged by Cézanne's rejection of its part in painting) in starting again from the beginning and rearranging everything prior to Picasso in order to face him and Matisse as well on their own ground. In the works on paper, in black and white and in colour, he worked with the same motifs and the same problems. Pollock started his investigation of drawing in black on white in a painting, *Number 32, 1950*[58] by isolating the non-descriptive black line, the line that is the trace of its own process. This line is in reality the line of figuration; in its non-objective phase it acts as a connective and carries the 'memory' of figuration, transcended, through to connect again to the figurative works. Pollock brings it back first to the description of edges and from there to the description of figures, as in *Echo* (1951).[59] He moves between figuration and abstraction, cursive contour that moves to non-objective line and simultaneously dissolves into non-objective marks of sensation, and then reconstitutes itself as a descriptive line. Sometimes the black floods the negative areas between forms, and at

55. Quoted by Lee Krasner Pollock in conversation with the author.

56. Picasso's *Guernica*, 1937, is at the root of modern ethical painting. Pollock's (and all advanced American) painting retained the emotional impact of this passionate statement, which was both a political and moral statement of outrage and a plastically advanced painting.

57. Handwritten note in the artist's file.

58. Kunstsammlung Nordrhein-Westfalen, Düsseldorf.

59. The Museum of Modern Art, New York. Acquired through the Lillie P. Bliss Bequest and the Mr and Mrs David Rockefeller Fund.

other times it intrudes to 'model' the figures. Again we have figures that have only the space of their own shadows, frequently rendered as kinetic sensations. Concentrating on the figure, Pollock plays with the old academic convention that drawing the figure in line precedes painting in colour; he has penetrated Matisse and Picasso and taken the automatic line back to cursive calligraphy and the 'classical' conception of contour drawing that unites the century. The small colour works on paper are the initial investigation of a new mode of colour painting that appears in the stained canvases of 1952–3.

Pollock's work recapitulates the problems stated at the beginning of the century. These problems and their solutions had been the basis for the beginning of a new art in Europe at the start of the century; they became the basis for a new art for the United States in the middle of the century. The new art was again a transformation, a kind of transcendent intensification of the old, to which it is both united and divided by a restatement in absolute terms of the common pictorial strategy that holds the century together. It is the availability of this heritage that marks the second half of the century.

Following from Pollock, the new point of structural reference became the all-over field. Jasper Johns wanted to restore the image to advanced art, but now any image had to be reconciled to the all-over field of advanced art as its condition for survival.[60] Johns seems to have decided that in order to reconcile image to an all-over field it was necessary for him to return to the same starting point as Pollock[61] and confront the same issues but make use of different referents; Johns, though, also initially drew inferences from Picasso's Analytic Cubist drawing, as well as from Seurat's shadow constructions, namely, that the depicted object is the structure and soul of the picture, and that it is constructed by its internal shadows. Johns's strategy became one of object identity and object illusionism and the kind of illusion proper to each class of object – the relation of objects to each other and to the prime object: the painting itself.

Johns began by depicting literally flat objects, flags and targets, and those which reinforced the illusion of flatness, numbers and the alphabet in modular series (not, for the moment, as words as in Cubism). Around 1960 he decided that the drawing sheet represented the flattest condition for illusion. 'His . . . area of investigation became the manner in which the illusionism of the page differed from that of the canvas',[62] restoring drawing, as such, to advanced art. But literal flatness was only one of the conditions of drawing: there was also the classical differentiation between line and colour. Drawing is linear; as it departs from an exclusively linear mode and moves into tonal modulation, to shadow, it mimics the effects of colour and becomes an analogy for colour rendering. Starting with linear sequences in 1957, Johns moved into tonal methods and the use of loose graphite suspended in a wash, charcoal, and other soft but monochromatic mediums through which ground light shines, binding illusion to surface. In fact, he began to investigate the perceptual illusion of drawing to its referent object and its analogous existence as an independent illusion of a painting. *Numbers* (1966) is characteristic in that it exists in numerous drawn, painted, printed, and even relief versions.

Johns's questioning of the basic relationships of tactile to colouristic perceptual illusions is a subtle restatement of the explorations of Seurat and Cézanne with reference to Impressionism and of Picasso with

60. Barbara Rose, 'The Graphic Work of Jasper Johns: Part I', *Artforum* (April 1970), p. 64.
61. Ibid.
62. Ibid., p. 67.

reference to both of them. Johns has grasped that shadow is the basis of illusion in the drawings of Seurat and Picasso. In Johns's drawing the shadow is integrated with the object, as the condition of its flatness, and then with the drawing stroke itself. In drawings such as *Numbers*, shadow conjures the images, the illusion. In earlier works Johns makes the object and the subject coexistent with each other as image and coextensive with the conditions of its illusion.

In later drawings such as *Voice* (1969) (fig. 102), illusion itself is the subject of the picture; its space the substance of shadow. To render these shadows, Johns at first resorts to a repetitive linear phrasing in a line that connects and disconnects and corresponds in its vertical and horizontal extensions to the internal divisions of the motif. Since the images are known to us in advance, we are dealing with a hand-crafted Readymade, just as the stenciled numbers are ready-made signs. We are at the start of another linear reorganisation, one in which the line, like Seurat's dots and van Gogh's contours, comprises a module, now thoroughly systematised. Seurat's massing of form out of value and contrast has been accommodated to the automatic line and the fast-and-loose brushwork of Abstract Expressionism, which has itself been reduced in scale. It finally gets broken down to objective parts, to component painterly strokes. In *Jubilee* (1960) the names of the colours are supplied for the tonal strokes. Unlike Seurat, Johns provides all the clues, as well as a solution in the related painting. We are also to participate in the colour experience of the drawing: the colour is named so that we can supply it, as Klee names the *Crooked Mouth and Light Green Eyes of Mrs. B.* (1925) (fig. 54), so that we can supply the green of her eyes.

We are part of an exquisite game, in which the whole tradition of twentieth-century art is part of the play, with the rules made up *ad hoc* by Johns himself, but always with reference to the art object as a perceptual field, coextensive with the artist's experience. And we move always in response to the artist's moves in this field. To return to *Voice*: the game is to draw the dissolved images out of the shadows, whence they may have been banished by the sweep of the wire with its bar of blank space, or, conversely, the sweeping device may itself be trying to elicit images, to give utterance to the unexpressed in the primordial ground of the shadow; this flickers as though it is a kind of palimpsest, erased ground twice used, trying to reveal its memories and secrets. *Voice* is also a kind of Braille, if it frustrates our voice and our sight, it also provokes and frustrates our touch – what will we use the fork for? We long to reach out and repeat the movement of the sweep. The spatial play is complex. The bar erasing the flat stenciled voice of the shadow is an empty area: it prevents the dissolution of the whole to a totally illusory field and restores the surface, as does the fork to some extent. Line dissolves here to the softness of a paint stroke and hardens to a wiry elegance. We are dealing with one of the master draughtsmen of the twentieth century, one who asserts drawing as a tone poem, a new mode.

Johns's initial concern in drawing had been with the condition of flat objects expressed as surface, fields contained by their object/subject identification. His later work is concerned with the expansion of the surface field beyond identification with specific objects, including the limited set of numbers or alphabet series. He achieves this extension by the creation of matched sets, groups of lines (which he expresses in colour as well as tone) at first interwoven like hatching (as in the background of *Savarin*, 1977) (fig. 103), and then organised into areas which have been likened to flagstones, rendering an infinitely extensible modular system by repetition and matching.

Initially the game was to extend the image by matching unrelated images (rendered as differently modulated linear sets) edge to edge. Eventually the suggestion was that one edge of the field could as easily be attached to its opposite edge. Gradually Johns became concerned with rendering a continuously curved surface as a flat closed field – surface – so that the field becomes in effect a world without end. If Johns's closed colour and tonal sets were rearranged and reattached according to the system given by matching repeated sets the suggestion is that they would open to represent a continuously curved surface. In this he relates to Cézanne's double system of colour and linear modulations which render both the shadow and contour of individual objects and express their attachment in an overall scheme that represents the pictorial surface as coextensive with the curved plane of vision. Johns sets us on much the same kind of stop-and-go search across and around the surface of the work. However, his method suggests openings and breaks in space that are purely conceptual. In this he joined the implications of his own initial explorations to contemporary concerns about the drawing as an expandable structure in a new alignment of object and illusion.

Johns projected the continuing investigation of art in terms of a new organisation of elements as modular and serial, and his investigation of object illusionism resulted in an insistence that a work of art was either three-dimensional (wholly objective) or flat (totally surface). Painting was seen as a kind of low relief, an illusion of a three-dimensional object. The three-dimensional object itself became an art of flat surfaces projected in space.

Johns's immediate contemporary, Robert Rauschenberg, had also taken up drawing as a primary means of expression, producing, in 1959–60, his extraordinary series of drawings inspired by Dante's *Inferno* (pl. XVI, figs. 98, 99). Based on a system of double illusion, the image is again conjured out of shadows, but the pre-existent images are three-dimensional ones already reduced to two dimensions. They represent a remarkable technical innovation, drawing by transfer process. Unlike Klee's transfers, Rauschenberg's are made from printed images, transferred to the drawing sheet by moistening them with lighter fluid and scrubbing them with a pencil whose scrawling line unites the pictorial surface. The drawings are a species of illusionary collage; the process enables Rauschenberg to achieve representational images without resorting to contour drawing. Yet the friction of the pencil in the application of the images re-introduces the autographic function of drawing within an apparently mechanistic context.

Johns and Rauschenberg made drawing as such available again to advanced art, and there followed an extraordinary florescence of drawing in the United States in the 1960s. Roy Lichtenstein and Claes Oldenburg addressed themselves to different aspects of the tradition of drawing: Lichtenstein, especially to the modern tradition and to contemporary popular drawing (drawing for comic strips and reproduction), and Oldenburg to a kind of paraphrase of 'high' art tradition (drawing as 'arty handwork'). For Oldenburg, a sculptor, one use of drawing became the confrontation of the human form, which he felt was not available to him as a subject for sculpture. His sculpture was primarily about objects, fragments of the everyday environment. The majority of his drawings were about the visualisation of these objects as they dominated the environment; they are impossible monumental projects representing for him a nostalgia for the grand tradition of sculpture, as well as drawing.

The system of rationalisation instigated by Johns and carried on in reaction to the absorption of the preliminary to the act of painting in Abstract Expressionism resulted in the idea of an art which projects the art object as a rule-dominated structure before it is a sculpture, a drawing or a painting. The work of art is seen as formed by a structural model that is verbally projected; a work of art made of generalised elements so basic that they could be exchanged *ad infinitum* within agreed rules, the rules constituting a kind of system, which in its application opened from one set of rules to another, and another, and so on. We see this especially in the art of Sol LeWitt, where the visual components follow from the need to find the simplest elements with which to form a structure that would fit the most elementary description of a visual work of art. The latter would then also have correspondence with other disciplines that were dominated by rules or projected by systems: in art, poetry and music (eventually rule-dominated systems would influence dance).

For LeWitt, art's primary creative aspect was that of the conception, therefore his art could then be executed by other people, following rules that were both specific yet sufficiently flexible to be applied in differing settings, without the artist's participation. Drawing was initially projected as the diagrammatic aspect of making a three-dimensional work and of placing it in three-dimensional space: LeWitt transferred the Cubist grid to the floor, creating a structure in three dimensions out of it. This structure, or variations of it, could then be repeated as modular elements for structures of a greater complexity or arrangements of multiple structures placed on the grid. Drawing itself was projected initially from this sculptural notation; it was then subjected to the same rule-making logic.

The first drawings were simply the four basic directions of lines, vertical, horizontal, diagonal right and diagonal left (these could be combined), repeated in close sequence within the confines of a progressively Cubist grid. These could then be combined and progressively superimposed one over another, beginning with vertical and horizontal, continuing through twenty-four basic permutations of one, two, three, four, and ending with a combination of all four. Four basic colours were established (red, blue, yellow, black), the primary colours of the spectrum. These were used only as line and followed the same rules.

In a brilliant act of intuition the drawing was transferred into space itself, onto the wall, where it became the ultimate work of flat surface illusion. It is important to emphasise that the projection onto the wall put the drawing into the same kind of space as the structures occupied, the available space of the world, interpreted in each case as the given room with its given walls. Thus the dialogue between the two-dimensional and the three-dimensional that had begun with Cubism was carried into space itself where the concerns of each were radically differentiated, although conceptually totally interdependent. The first full wall drawing followed the same system: it was the simplest possible expression of the concept. 'Lines in four directions (horizontal, vertical, diagonal left, and diagonal right) covering the entire surface of the wall.

Note: the lines are drawn with hard graphite (8H or 9H) as close together as possible ($\frac{1}{16}$ in apart approximately) and are straight.'[63]

The wall drawing, limited at first to a small area of the wall, quickly spread to the limits of the given wall itself, the surface giving reflected light from space itself. The component of the field was now simply the most elemental unit of illusionism — the line that does not exist in nature. Representation was excluded (at least initially); the object existed only in space, drawing was an expression of surface, flat tactility, yet paradoxically dissolved to ambient space in pure chiascuro light and shadow or coloured light. The permutations of kinds of lines were multiplied and varied by LeWitt — long, short, irregular, randomly placed; in some drawings the rules were incorporated into the drawing itself and written directly on the wall. Eventually, depiction of the object came back to the wall. Simple descriptions of geometric figures, which were also the objects of his sculpture, were also depicted in white chalk on black ground and, finally, over monochromatic colour grounds. Thus, the statement of the basic structures of twentieth-century art was rendered in the simplest possible terms, and as a form of mediation between two- and three-dimensional concerns, between verbal and visual, a recognition of the language of drawing.

63. Sol LeWitt, 'Paragraphs on Conceptual Art', *Artforum* (June 1967), pp. 79–80.

Dates enclosed in parentheses do not appear on the works themselves. All works are on paper unless otherwise indicated. Sheet dimensions are given in millimetres, height preceding width. Where a work is illustrated, the colour plate number or figure number appears at the end of the catalogue entry.

Carl Andre

American, born 1935.

1 *Crowding* (1965)
Cut-and-pasted paper on cardboard. 285 × 143 mm. Gift of Carol O. Selle. 700.76. Fig. 107

2 *Impulse Driver* (1965)
Cut-and-pasted paper and pen and ink on cardboard. 134 × 199 mm. Acquired with matching funds from the Lydia K. and Harry L. Winston Art Collection and the National Endowment for the Arts. 478.76.

Alexander Archipenko

American, born Ukraine. 1887–1964. In Paris 1908–21; to United States 1923.

3 *Figure in Movement* 1913
Cut-and-pasted paper, crayon and pencil. 476 × 314 mm. Gift of the Perls Galleries, New York. 806.69. Fig. 40

Jean (originally Hans) Arp

French, born Alsace. 1887–1966. In Switzerland 1959–66.

4 *Automatic Drawing* 1916
Brush and ink on grey paper. 426 × 540 mm. Given anonymously. 109.36. Fig. 74

5 *Arrangement According to the Laws of Chance (Collage with Squares)* (1916–17)
Torn-and-pasted papers. 485 × 346 mm. Purchase. 457.37.

Lawrence Atkinson

British, 1873–1931.

6 *Composition* (c. 1914)
Pencil and pastel. 803 × 551 mm. The Joan and Lester Avnet Collection. 3.78. Fig. 28

Giacomo Balla

Italian, 1871–1958.

7 Study for *Street Light* (1909)
Pencil. 142 × 277 mm. Christopher Tietze Fund. 2659.67.

8 Study for *Street Light* (1909)
Pencil. 220 × 180 mm. Mrs Bertram Smith Fund. 2660.67a. Fig. 35

Balthus (Baltusz Klossowski de Rola)

French, born 1908.

9 *Reclining Nude* (1967)
Charcoal. 500 × 698 mm. Gift of Mr and Mrs Donald B. Straus. 2357.67. Fig. 105

Max Beckmann

German, 1884–1950. In Amsterdam 1936–47; in United States 1947–50.

10 *The Prodigal Son among Swine* (1921)
Gouache, watercolour and traces of pencil on parchment. 364 × 298 mm. Purchase. 266.39.

11 *The Return of the Prodigal Son* (1921)
Gouache, watercolour and traces of pencil on parchment. 364 × 298 mm. Purchase. 265.39. Fig. 61

Umberto Boccioni

Italian, 1882–1916.

12 Study for *The City Rises* 1910
Crayon, chalk and charcoal. 588 × 867 mm. Mrs Simon Guggenheim Fund. 371.61.

13 *States of Mind: The Farewells* (1911)
Charcoal and chalk. 584 × 863 mm. Gift of Vico Baer. 522.41. Fig. 37

Constantin Brancusi

French, born Rumania. 1876–1957. To Paris 1904.

14 *The First Step* (1913)
Crayon. 821 × 380 mm. Benjamin Scharps and David Scharps Fund. 1.56. Fig. 30

15 *View of the Artist's Studio* 1918
Gouache and pencil. 328 × 411 mm. The Joan and Lester Avnet Collection. 19.78. Fig. 31

Georges Braque

French, 1882–1963.

16 *Still Life with Letters* (1914)

Cut-and-pasted papers, charcoal, and pastel. 517 × 730 mm. The Joan and Lester Avnet Collection. 20.78. Fig. 27

Carlo Carrà

Italian, 1881–1966.

17 *Ritmi Plastici* 1911

Pen and ink. 107 × 74 mm. The Joan and Lester Avnet Fund. 703.80. Fig. 36

Paul Cézanne

French, 1839–1906.

18 *The Bridge at Gardanne* (1885–86)

Watercolour and pencil. 206 × 311 mm. Lillie P. Bliss Collection. 6.34a.

19 *Mercury after Pigalle (Le Mercure de Pigalle)* (c. 1890)

Pencil. 380 × 278 mm. The Joan and Lester Avnet Fund. 463.80.

20 *Foliage* (1895–1900)

Watercolour and pencil. 448 × 568 mm. Lillie P. Bliss Collection. 9.34a. Plate II

21 *Rocky Ridge above Le Château Noir* (1895–1900)

Watercolour and pencil. 317 × 476 mm. Lillie P. Bliss Collection. 21.34.

Marc Chagall

French, born Russia 1887. To France 1923; in United States 1941–8.

22 *Golgotha* 1912

Gouache, watercolour and pencil. 474 × 592 mm. The Joan and Lester Avnet Collection. 24.78. Fig. 39

23 *Homage to Gogol* 1917

Watercolour. 394 × 502 mm. Acquired through the Lillie P. Bliss Bequest. 71.44.

Salvador Dali

Spanish, born 1904. Active in Paris and New York.

24 *Untitled* 1927

Pen and brush and ink. 251 × 326 mm. Gift of Mrs Alfred R. Stern in honour of René d'Harnoncourt. 202.72. Fig. 75

Stuart Davis

American, 1894–1964.

25 *Composition No. 5* (1932)

Gouache. 559 × 759 mm. Gift of Abby Aldrich Rockefeller. 50.35. Fig. 90

Robert Delaunay

French, 1885–1941.

26 *The Tower* (1911 inscribed 1910)

Pen and ink and traces of pencil on brown cardboard. 539 × 489 mm. Abby Aldrich Rockefeller Fund. 235.35. Fig. 24

27 *The Tower and the Wheel* (1913 inscribed 1909/10)

Brush and pen and ink. 647 × 497 mm. Abby Aldrich Rockefeller Fund. 234.35.

Paul Delvaux

Belgian, born 1897.

28 *The Siesta* 1947

Watercolour and pen and ink. 595 × 783 mm. Kay Sage Tanguy Bequest. 342.63. Fig. 84

André Derain

French, 1880–1954.

29 *Three Dancers (Bacchic Dance)* (1906)

Watercolour and pencil. 495 × 648 mm. Gift of Abby Aldrich Rockefeller. 61.35. Plate III

Jim Dine

American, born 1935.

30 *Five-bladed Saw* (from *Seven Untitled Drawings*) 1973

Charcoal and graphite. 651 × 502 mm. Gift of the Robert Lehman Foundation, Inc. 484.76.1. Fig. 100

31 *Hoof Nipper* (from *Seven Untitled Drawings*) 1973

Charcoal and graphite. 651 × 502 mm. Gift of the Robert Lehman Foundation, Inc. 484.76.6.

32 *Oil Can* (from *Seven Untitled Drawings*) 1973

Charcoal and graphite. 651 × 502 mm. Gift of the Robert Lehman Foundation, Inc. 484.76.7.

33 *Second Baby Drawing* 1976

Charcoal, crayon, and oil. 1011 × 775 mm. Gift of Lily Auchincloss. 13.77. Fig. 101

Otto Dix

German, 1891–1969.

34 *Café Couple* 1921
Watercolour and pencil. 508 × 410 mm. Purchase.
124.45. Fig. 60

Theo van Doesburg (C. E. M. Kupper)

Dutch, 1883–1931.

35 Four studies for *Composition (The Cow)*
(1916)
Pencil. 117 × 159 mm; or 159 × 117 mm. Purchase.
227.48. Fig. 48

36 *Composition (The Cow)* 1916
Tempera, oil and charcoal. 397 × 577 mm.
Purchase. 226.48. Fig. 49

Oscar Dominguez

French. born Spain. 1906–57. To Paris 1927.

37 Untitled 1936
Gouache transfer (decalcomania). 359 × 252 mm.
Purchase. 458.37. Fig. 77

Jean Dubuffet

French, born 1901.

38 *Joe Bousquet in Bed* (January) 1947
Gouache and ink over gesso incised with pen.
494 × 323 mm. Mrs Simon Guggenheim Fund. 15.69.
Fig. 83

39 *Nude (Corps de Dame)* (November) 1950
Pen and reed pen and ink. 270 × 212 mm. The Joan
and Lester Avnet Collection. 54.78.

40 *Epidermis* (October–November) 1960
Ink imprint. 505 × 672 mm. Gift of the artist in
honour of Mr and Mrs Ralph F. Colin. 1316.68.

Marcel Duchamp

American, born France. 1887–1968. In United
States 1915–18, 1920–23, 1942–68.

41 *Handmade Stereopticon Slide* (1918–19)
Pencil on stereopticon slide. 57 × 57 mm, each
image. Katherine S. Dreier Bequest. 152.53.

42 *Monte Carlo Bond* (1924)
Photocollage on coloured lithograph. 311 × 197 mm.
Gift of the artist. 3.39. Fig. 73

Jacob Epstein

British, born United States. 1880–1959. To England
1905.

43 *Rock Driller* (c. 1913)
Conté crayon. 696 × 438 mm. The Joan and Lester
Avnet Collection. 78.78.

Max Ernst

French, born Germany. 1891–1976. To France
1922; in United States 1941–50.

44 *Alcohodada* (1919)
Pencil. 449 × 334 mm. John S. Newberry Fund.
819.69. Fig. 65

45 *Here Everything Is Still Floating* (1920)
Pasted photoengravings and pencil. 105 × 124 mm.
Purchase. 282.37. Fig. 71

46 *The Horse, He's Sick* (1920)
Pasted photoengravings and pencil. 146 × 216 mm.
Abby Aldrich Rockefeller Fund. 241.35. Fig. 72

Exquisite Corpse

(composite drawing, top to bottom: Yves Tanguy,
Joan Miró, Max Morise, Man Ray).

47 *Nude* (1926–7)
Pen and ink, pencil and coloured crayons.
362 × 229 mm. Purchase. 260.35.

Exquisite Corpse

(composite drawing, top to bottom: Esteban Francés,
Remedios Lissaraga, Oscar Dominguez, Marcel Jean).

48 Untitled (1935)
Cut-and-pasted papers. 276 × 208 mm. F. M.
Hirschland Fund. 14.69. Fig. 76

Lyonel Feininger

American, 1871–1956. In Germany 1887–1936; in
United States 1937–56.

49 *Ruin by the Sea II* 1934
Watercolour and pen and ink. 302 × 490 mm. Gift of
Julia Feininger. 99.63. Fig. 53

Sam Francis (Samuel Lewis Francis)

American, born 1923. In France 1950–60.

50 Untitled (1958)
Watercolour. 687 × 1017 mm. Gift of the Udo M.
Reinach Estate. 28.60. Fig. 97

Paul Gauguin

French, 1848–1903. In Tahiti and Marquesas Islands 1891–3, 1895–1903.

51 *Jacob Meyer de Haan* (1889)
Watercolour and traces of pencil. 164 × 115 mm. Gift of Arthur G. Altschul. 699.76.

Alberto Giacometti

Swiss, 1901–66. To Paris 1922.

52 *Head of a Woman* 1923
Pencil. 302 × 230 mm. Anonymous extended loan. 81.576. Fig. 34

Vincent van Gogh

Dutch, 1853–90. To France 1886.

53 *Street at Saintes-Maries* (1888)
Brush and reed pen and ink and traces of pencil. 245 × 318 mm. Abby Aldrich Rockefeller Bequest. 243.48. Fig. 1

54 *Hospital Corridor at Saint-Rémy* (May–early June 1889)
Gouache and watercolour. 613 × 473 mm. Abby Aldrich Rockefeller Bequest. 242.48. Plate 1

Arshile Gorky (Vosdanig Manoog Adoian)

American, born Turkish Armenia. 1904–1948. To United States 1920.

55 *Portrait of Vartoosh* (Vartoosh Adoian Mooradian) (1935)
Pencil. 312 × 241 mm. Kay Sage Tanguy Bequest (by exchange). 429.75. Fig. 92

56 Study for *Summation* 1946
Pencil and coloured chalks. 470 × 618 mm. The Sidney and Harriet Janis Collection (fractional gift). 605.67. Fig. 93

Juan Gris (José Victoriano González)

Spanish, 1887–1927. To France 1906.

57 *Still Life with Bottle and Funnel* (1911)
Pencil. 479 × 316 mm. Alva Gimbel Fund. 401.70. Fig. 25

58 *Breakfast* (1914)
Pasted papers, crayon and oil on canvas. 809 × 597 mm. Acquired through the Lillie P. Bliss Bequest. 248.48. Plate VII

59 *Max Jacob* 1919
Pencil. 365 × 267 mm. Gift of James Thrall Soby. 84.58.

George Grosz

American, 1893–1959. Born and died in Germany. In United States 1932–59.

60 *Dispute by Moonlight* (c. 1920)
Brush and India ink. 676 × 498 mm. A. Conger Goodyear Fund. 4.48a-b. Fig. 62

61 *The Engineer Heartfield* (1920)
Watercolour, pasted postcard, and halftone. 419 × 305 mm. Gift of A. Gonger Goodyear. 176.52. Plate X

62 *Methuselah* (1922)
Watercolour, metallic paint, and pen and ink. 526 × 411 mm. Mr and Mrs Werner E. Josten Fund. 143.57. Fig. 63

63 *Circe* 1927
Watercolour. 660 × 486 mm. Gift of Mr and Mrs Walter Bareiss and an anonymous donor (by exchange). 73.81. Fig. 64

Erich Heckel

German, 1883–1970.

64 *Girl Reading (Young Girl)* 1912
Charcoal pencil. 502 × 355 mm. The Estée and Joseph Lauder Foundation Fund. 106.74. Fig. 57

Hannah Hoch

German, 1889–1978.

65 *Man and Machine* (1921)
Watercolour and traces of pencil. 290 × 242 mm. The Joan and Lester Avnet Collection. 102.78. Fig. 69

Edward Hopper

American, 1882–1978.

66 *Box Factory, Gloucester* (1928)
Watercolour. 356 × 508 mm. Gift of Abby Aldrich Rockefeller. 85.35. Fig. 89

Jasper Johns

American, born 1930.

67 *Jubilee* (1960)
Brush and graphite wash and pencil. 711 × 533 mm. The Joan and Lester Avnet Collection. 105.78.

68 *Numbers* 1966
Pencil and brush and graphite wash on brown paper.
658 × 548 mm. Gift of Mrs Bliss Parkinson in honour
of René d'Harnoncourt. 18.69.

69 *Voice* 1969
Brush and graphite wash. 718 × 521 mm. Purchase.
76.81. Fig. 102

70 *Savarin* 1977
Brush and pen and ink on plastic sheet.
921 × 664 mm. Gift of The Lauder Foundation.
103.79. Fig. 103

Wassily Kandinsky

Russian, 1866–1944. Worked in Germany and
France.

71 Study for *Painting with White Form*
(1913)
Watercolour and ink. 276 × 381 mm. Katherine S.
Dreier Bequest. 157.53. Fig. 52

72 Untitled 1915
Pen and ink. 228 × 232 mm. Purchase. 398.41.

73 *The Horseman* 1916
Watercolour, wash, brush and ink, and pencil.
323 × 249 mm. The Joan and Lester Avnet Collection.
106.78.

74 *Black Relationship* 1924
Watercolour and pen and ink. 368 × 362 mm.
Acquired through the Lillie P. Bliss Bequest. 341.49.
Plate XII

75 *Round Poetry* 1933
Watercolour and pen and ink. 441 × 441 mm. John S.
Newberry Fund. 1518.68.

Ernst Ludwig Kirchner

German, 1890–1938.
76 *Street Scene. Berlin* (1914)
Brush and ink. 546 × 394 mm. Gift of Curt Valentin.
330.41. Fig. 58

Paul Klee

German, 1879–1940. Born and died in Switzerland.
77 *Laughing Gothic* 1915
Watercolour and traces of pencil. 260 × 136 mm.
Purchase. 91.50. Plate VIII

78 *The Angler* 1921
Watercolour on transfer drawing. 476 × 312 mm.
John S. Newberry Collection. 64.61.

79 *The Crooked Mouth and Light Green Eyes
of Mrs B.* 1925
Pen and ink and dry brush. 165 × 362 mm.
A. Conger Goodyear Fund. 94.50. Fig. 54

80 *Early Morning in Ro . . .* 1925
Watercolour. 370 × 509 mm. Gift of Mrs Gertrud A.
Mellon. 1262.64.

81 *Man with Top Hat* 1925
Gouache and pen and ink on paper over cardboard.
383 × 270 mm. Given anonymously. 570.64.

82 *Magicians in Dispute* 1928
Pen and ink. 393 × 597 mm. Mr and Mrs William B.
Jaffe Fund. 196.55.

83 *Aged Dwarf* 1933
Gouache. 328 × 210 mm. The Joan and Lester Avnet
Collection. 110.78a.

84 *Lady Apart* 1940
Brush and ink. 416 × 295 mm. A. Conger Goodyear
Fund. 96.50. Fig. 55

Gustav Klimt

Austrian, 1862–1918.
85 *Woman in Profile* (1898–9)
Blue pencil. 427 × 287 mm. The Joan and Lester
Avnet Collection. 910.79.

Oskar Kokoschka

British, born Austria. 1886–1980. In England
1938–53; to Switzerland 1953.
86 *Nude with Back* (c. 1907)
Watercolour, crayon, pencil, and pen and ink.
451 × 311 mm. Rose Gershwin Fund. 549.54. Fig. 56

Willem de Kooning

American, born The Netherlands, 1904. To United
States 1926.
87 *Standing Woman* (1952)
Cut-and-pasted paper, pastel, and pencil.
303 × 241 mm. The Lauder Foundation Fund. 33.75.
Plate XIV

88 *Woman XI* (1961)
Oil and pastel on paper mounted on canvas. 735 × 566 mm. The Sidney and Harriet Janis Collection. 623.67.

Alfred Kubin
Austrian, 1877–1959.
89 *The Stealthy Watcher* (c. 1903)
Wash and pen and ink. 214 × 221 mm. John S. Newberry Fund. 2373.67.

František (or Frank) Kupka
Czech, 1871–1957. To France 1895.
90 *Study with Green* (c. 1912)
Chalk and gouache. 191 × 245 mm. John S. Newberry Fund. 830.69.

91 Study for *Amorpha: Fugue in Two Colours* (1912)
Tempera and brush and ink. 214 × 225 mm. Gift of Mr and Mrs Frantisek Kupka. 569.56.15.

Michael Larionov
Russian, 1881–1964. To Paris 1915.
92 *Rayonist Composition Number 8* (1912–13)
Brush and ink, gouache, and watercolour. 508 × 375 mm. Gift of the artist. 40.36.

Bart Anthony van der Leck
Dutch, 1876–1958.
93 Untitled (1917)
Gouache and pencil. 447 × 571 mm. Gift of Constance B. Cartwright. 149.73. Fig. 50

Fernand Léger
French, 1881–1955. In United States 1940–45.
94 *Verdun, The Trench Diggers* (December 1916)
Watercolour. 359 × 263 mm. Frank Crowninshield Fund. 142.44. Fig. 29

95 *Circus Family* 1941
Brush and ink. 1035 × 891 mm. Gift of William H. Weintraub. 502.64.

96 *Face and Hands* 1952
Brush and ink and touches of pencil. 660 × 501 mm. Mrs Wendell T. Bush Fund. 18.53. Fig. 91

Sol LeWitt
American, born 1928.
97 *Plan for Wall Drawing* 1969
Pen and ink and pencil. 527 × 526 mm. D. S. and R. H. Gottesman Foundation Fund. 1019.69. Fig. 108

98 *Straight Lines in Four Directions Superimposed* (September 1969)
Graphite on white wall. Size variable. Purchase. 1347.74.

Roy Lichtenstein
American, born 1923.
99 *Tablet* 1966
Pencil and tusche. 762 × 559 mm. Anonymous extended loan.

Jacques Lipchitz
American, born Lithuania. 1891–1973. In France 1909–41; to United States 1941.
100 *Girl with Braided Hair* (1914)
Pencil. 199 × 158 mm. Mr and Mrs Milton J. Petrie Fund. 296.74. Fig. 32

101 *Seated Nude* (1915)
Crayon, charcoal, pencil, watercolour, and brush and ink. 499 × 328 mm. The Joan and Lester Avnet Collection. 126.78.

El Lissitzky (Lazar Markovich Lissitzky)
Russian, 1890–1941. In Germany 1921–3, 1925–8.
102 Study for page for *A Suprematist Story about Two Squares in 6 Constructions* (1920)
Watercolour and pencil on cardboard. 256 × 202 mm. The Sidney and Harriet Janis Collection. 628.67. Fig. 44

103 *Proun GK* (c. 1922)
Gouache, brush and ink, and pencil. 660 × 502 mm. 444.81.

Kasimir Malevich
Russian, 1878–1935. In Germany 1927.
104 *Suprematist Element: Circle* (1915)
Pencil. 470 × 365 mm. 808.35.

105 *Suprematist Elements: Squares* (1915)
Pencil. 502 × 358 mm. 807.35. Fig. 41

Man Ray (Emmanuel Radenski)

American, 1890–1976. To Paris 1921.

106 *Admiration of the Orchestrelle for the Cinematograph* 1919
Gouache, wash, and ink, airbrushed. 660 × 546 mm. Gift of A. Conger Goodyear. 231.37. Fig. 67

Franz Marc

German, 1880–1916.

107 *Blue Horse with Rainbow* (1913)
Gouache, watercolour, and pencil. 162 × 257 mm. John S. Newberry Collection. 2.64. Fig. 51

John Marin

American, 1870–1953. In Paris 1905–10.

108 *Lower Manhattan (Composing Derived from Top of Woolworth)* 1922
Watercolour and charcoal with paper cut-out attached with thread. 549 × 683 mm. Acquired through the Lillie P. Bliss Bequest. 143.45. Fig. 86

Agnes Martin

American, born Canada 1912. To United States 1933.

109 *Untitled* 1960
Pen and ink. 302 × 306 mm. Acquired with matching funds from The Lauder Foundation and the National Endowment for the Arts. 107.79. Fig. 106

110 *Red Bird* (1964)
Pen and ink. 311 × 305 mm. Gift of Mrs Bliss Parkinson. 159.66.

111 *Stone* (1964)
Pencil and pen and ink. 279 × 279 mm. Eugene and Clare Thaw Fund. 606.64.

André Masson

French, born 1896. In United States 1941–5.

112 *Werewolf* (1944)
Brush and ink and pastel on green paper. 457 × 610 mm. Acquired through the Lillie P. Bliss Bequest. 126.44. Fig. 82

Henri Matisse

French, 1869–1954.

113 *Jeanne Manguin* (1906)
Brush and ink. 622 × 469 mm. Given anonymously. 17.68. Fig. 6

114 *The Plumed Hat* (1919)
Pencil. 540 × 365 mm. Gift of The Lauder Foundation. 422.75. Fig. 7

115 *Reclining Nude* (1927)
Pen and ink. 277 × 320 mm. The Tisch Foundation, Inc. Fund. 297.74. Fig. 8

116 *Reclining Nude* 1938
Charcoal. 605 × 813 mm. Purchase. 79.81. Fig. 9

117 *Dahlias and Pomegranates* 1947
Brush and ink. 764 × 565 mm. Abby Aldrich Rockefeller Fund. 12.50. Fig. 10

118 *The Necklace (Nude with a Necklace)* May 1950
Brush and ink. 528 × 407 mm. The Joan and Lester Avnet Collection. 131.78. Fig. 11

Matta (Sebastian Antonio Matta Echaurren)

Chilean, born 1912. In United States 1939–48. Lives in Paris.

119 *Untitled* 1942
Pencil and crayon. 486 × 612 mm. The James Thrall Soby Bequest. 914.79. Fig. 81

Joan Miró

Spanish, born 1893. In Paris 1919–40.

120 *Statue* May 1926
Conté crayon. 623 × 476 mm. Purchase. 86.36.

121 *Cartoon (final study)* for *Dutch Interior, I* (Summer 1928)
Charcoal and pencil. 626 × 473 mm. Gift of the artist. 126.73. Fig. 78

122 Study for *Painting* 11 February, 1933
Cut-and-pasted photomechanical reproductions and pencil. 468 × 630 mm. Gift of the artist. 131.73.

123 *Collage* 20 January, 1934
Corrugated cardboard, felt, gouache, and pencil on sandpaper. 369 × 236 mm. The James Thrall Soby Bequest. 109.79. Fig. 79

124 *The Beautiful Bird Revealing the Unknown to a Pair of Lovers* 1941
Gouache and oil wash. 457 × 381 mm. Acquired through the Lillie P. Bliss Bequest. 7.45. Plate XIII

Amedeo Modigliani

Italian, 1884–1920. To France 1906.

125 *Woman in Profile* (1910–11)
Charcoal. 429 × 267 mm. The Joan and Lester Avnet Collection. 134.78.

126 *Seated Nude* (1914)
Watercolour, wash, and pencil. 540 × 416 mm. Gift of Mrs Saidie A. May. 29.32. Fig. 33

Laszlo Moholy-Nagy

American, born Hungary. 1895–1946. In Germany 1921–34; to United States 1937.

127 *Chute* 1923
Collage of halftone reproductions of photographs, airbrush, and pen and ink. 648 × 495 mm. Gift of Mrs Sibyl Moholy-Nagy. 19.65. Fig. 68

Piet Mondrian

Dutch, 1872–1944. In Paris 1912–14, 1919–38; in New York 1940–44.

128 *Church Facade* (1914 inscribed 1912)
Charcoal. 990 × 634 mm. The Joan and Lester Avnet Collection. 137.78. Fig. 45

129 Study for *Broadway Boogie Woogie* 1942
Charcoal. 232 × 232 mm. Extended loan from Mr and Mrs Arnold Newman. EL 1977. 1347. Fig. 46

130 Study for *Broadway Boogie Woogie II* 1942
Charcoal. 229 × 232 mm. Extended loan from Mr and Mrs Arnold Newman. EL 1977. 1348. Fig. 47

Henry Moore

British, born 1898.

131 *Women Winding Wool* 1949
Crayon and watercolour. 348 × 636 mm. Gift of Mr and Mrs John A. Pope in honour of Paul J. Sachs. 244.62. Fig. 85

Robert Morris

American, born 1931.

132 *Blind Time XIII* 1973
Graphite. 892 × 1172 mm. Acquired with matching funds from The Lily Auchincloss Foundation and the National Endowment for the Arts. 299.74. Fig. 110

Bruce Nauman

American, born 1941.

133 *Face Mask* 1981
Charcoal, pastel and pencil. 1340 × 97 mm. Gift of The Lauder Foundation (1982). TR 5210. Fig. 112

Emil Nolde (Emil Hansen)

Danish, born North Schleswig, Germany, later part of Denmark. 1867–1956. Worked in Germany.

134 *Magicians* (1931–35)
Watercolour. 511 × 365 mm. Purchase. 654.39. Fig. 59

Georgia O'Keeffe

American, born 1887.

135 *Train at Night in the Desert* (1916)
Watercolour and touches of pencil. 303 × 206 mm. Acquired with matching funds from the Committee on Drawings and the National Endowment for the Arts. 113.79.

136 *Banana Flower* (1933)
Charcoal. 552 × 375 mm. Given anonymously (by exchange). 21.36. Fig. 87

Claes Oldenburg

American, born Sweden 1929. To United States 1936.

137 Study for *Dropped Cup of Coffee* 1967
Pencil, crayon, and wash. 765 × 564 mm. Gift of the artist. 2217.67.

138 Preliminary study for *Image of the Buddha Preaching* 1967
Pencil. 764 × 561 mm. Gift of Mr and Mrs Richard E. Oldenburg. 20.68. Fig. 104

Francis Picabia

French, 1879–1953. In New York 1913–17.

139 *New York* (1913)
Gouache, watercolour, and pencil. 558 × 759 mm. The Joan and Lester Avnet Collection. 145.78. Fig. 26

140 *Dada Movement* 1919
Pen and ink. 511 × 362 mm. Purchase. 285.37. Fig. 66

Pablo Picasso

Spanish, 1881–1973. To France 1904.

141 *Brooding Woman* (1904)
Watercolour. 267 × 366 mm. Gift of Mr and Mrs
Werner E. Josten. 4.56a. Fig. 13

142 *Sleeping Head* (late 1906) Study for *Les
Demoiselles d'Avignon.*
Watercolour. 224 × 175 mm. John S. Newberry
Collection. 383. 60. Fig. 14

143 *Head of the Medical Student* (Spring
1907) Study for *Les Demoiselles d'Avignon.*
Gouache and watercolour. 603 × 470 mm. A. Conger
Goodyear Fund. 14.52. Plate IV

144 *Bathers in a Forest* 1908
Watercolour and pencil on paper, mounted on canvas.
475 × 587 mm. Hillman Periodicals Fund. 28.57.
Fig. 15

145 *Sheet of Studies* (late 1908)
Brush and pen and ink. 320 × 494 mm. A. Conger
Goodyear Fund. 22.68.

146 *Head* (Spring 1909)
Gouache. 610 × 457 mm. Gift of Saidie A. May. 12.30.
Fig. 16

147 *The Mill at Horta* (Summer 1909)
Watercolour. 248 × 382 mm. The Joan and Lester
Avnet Collection. 149.78.

148 *Mlle Léonie* (1911–12)
Pen and ink. 305 × 197 mm. Anonymous extended
loan. 1982. 55. Fig. 19

149 *Cubist Study* (1912)
Brush and ink. 184 × 133 mm. Gift of Pierre Loeb.
753.43. Fig. 17

150 *Study for a Construction* (1912)
Pen and ink. 172 × 124 mm. Purchase. 754.43.
Fig. 18

151 *Study for a Construction* (1912)
Pen and ink. 172 × 127 mm. Purchase. 80.81.

152 *Guitar* Spring 1913
Charcoal, wax, crayon, ink and pasted papers.
664 × 496 mm. Nelson A. Rockefeller Bequest.
967.79. Plate VI

153 *Head* (Spring 1913)
Cut-and-pasted papers, pen and ink, pencil, and
watercolour. 429 × 287 mm. The Sidney and Harriet
Janis Collection. 640.67. Fig. 20

154 *Man in a Melon Hat* 1914
Pencil. 328 × 254 mm. John S. Newberry Collection.
385.60. Fig. 21

155 *Ricciotto Canudo* 1918
Pencil. 354 × 262 mm. Acquired through the Lillie P.
Bliss Bequest. 18.51.

156 *Nessus and Dejanira* 12 September 1920
Pencil. 209 × 260 mm. Acquired through the Lillie P.
Bliss Bequest. 184.52. Fig. 22

157 *Two Figures on a Beach* 28 July 1933
Pen and ink. 400 × 508 mm. Purchase. 655.39.
Fig. 23

158 *The Cock* 23 March 1938
Charcoal. 769 × 569 mm. Anonymous promised gift.

Jackson Pollock

American, 1912–56.

159 Untitled (*c.* 1950)
Ink. 444 × 565 mm. Anonymous extended loan.
Fig. 95

160 Untitled (1951)
Black and sepia ink with green gouache on mulberry
paper. 635 × 997 mm. Purchase (1982). TR 5148.7.

161 Untitled (1951)
Black and coloured inks on mulberry paper.
615 × 864 mm. The Joan and Lester Avnet
Collection. 153.78. Plate XV

162 Untitled (*c.* 1952)
Black ink and gouache on Howell paper.
450 × 565 mm. Gift of Lee Krasner Pollock in
memory of Jackson Pollock (1982). TR 5148.8.

Robert Rauschenberg

American, born 1925.

163 Thirty-four illustrations for Dante's *Inferno* (1959–60)

Combined drawings. Each sheet approximately 368 × 291 mm. Given anonymously. 346.63.1–34. The following are illustrated: Canto IV, fig. 98; Canto XIV, fig. 99; Canto XXXI, plate XVI.

Odilon Redon

French, 1860–1916.

164 *The Masque of the Red Death* (1883)

Charcoal on brown paper. 437 × 358 mm. The John S. Newberry Collection. 18.62. Fig. 4

165 *Dream Polyps* (c. 1885)

Charcoal, charcoal pencil and black chalk. 484 × 357 mm. Gift of Mr and Mrs Donald B. Straus. 279.73.

166 *The Accused* (1886)

Charcoal. 533 × 372 mm. Acquired through the Lillie P. Bliss Bequest. 199.52. Fig. 5

Dorothea Rockburne

Canadian.

167 *Copal No. 8* 1976

Kraft paper, blue pencil, glue and (copal) varnish. 740 × 994 mm. Gift of the Gilman Foundation. 173.77. Fig. 111

Alexander Rodchenko

Russian, 1891–1956.

168 *Composition* 1918

Gouache. 330 × 162 mm. Gift of the artist. 28.36. Fig. 43

Auguste Rodin

French, 1840–1917.

169 *Kneeling Man* (c. 1900)

Watercolour and pencil. 311 × 196 mm. Gift of Mr and Mrs Patrick Dinehart. 218.63.

170 *Nude with Serpent* (c. 1900–1905)

Watercolour and pencil. 320 × 247 mm. Gift of Mr and Mrs Patrick Dinehart. 217.63.

James Rosenquist

American, born 1933.

171 *White Spot* 1972

Pencil and crayon. 565 × 769 mm. Anonymous extended loan. 81.574.

Mark Rothko

American, born Latvia. 1903–70. To United States 1913.

172 *Archaic Idol* (1945)

Wash, pen and brush and ink, and gouache. 556 × 762 mm. The Joan and Lester Avnet Collection. 157.78a. Fig. 94

Georges Rouault

French, 1871–1958.

173 *Circus Act* 1905

Watercolour, pastel, charcoal, and brush and ink. 260 × 343 mm. The Joan and Lester Avnet Collection. 158.78.

174 *The Procuress (Woman at a Table)* 1906

Watercolour and pastel on cardboard. 308 × 242 mm. Acquired through the Lillie P. Bliss Bequest. 503.41. Fig. 12

Olga Rozanova

Russian, 1886–1918.

175 *The Universal War* 1916

Cut-and -pasted papers on grey paper. 407 × 311 mm. Purchase (1982). TR 5201. Fig. 42

Egon Schiele

Austrian, 1890–1918.

176 *Woman Wrapped in a Blanket* 1911

Watercolour and pencil. 447 × 311 mm. The Joan and Lester Avnet Collection. 161.78. Plate V

Oskar Schlemmer

German, 1888–1943.

177 Study for *The Triadic Ballet* (c. 1921–23)

Gouache, ink, and collage of photographs. 575 × 371 mm. Gift of Lily Auchincloss. 24.56. Fig. 70

Kurt Schwitters

British, born Germany. 1887–1948. To England 1940.

178 *Merz 252: Coloured Squares (Farbige Quadrate)* 1921

Collage of cut papers and pencil. 274 × 210 mm. The Sidney and Harriet Janis Collection. 649.67.

179 *Merz 460: Two Underdrawers* 1921

Collage of coloured cut papers, ribbon, printed cotton, and sweet wrapper. 204 × 172 mm. Katherine S. Dreier Bequest. 194.53.

180 *Merz: Santa Claus* 1922

Collage of papers and cloth. 284 × 208 mm. Purchase. 258.35. Plate XI

Richard Serra

American, born 1939.

181 *Heir* (1973)

Charcoal and synthetic acrylic polymer paint. 2912 × 1072 mm. Acquired with matching funds from Mr and Mrs S. I. Newhouse, Jr and the National Endowment for the Arts. 122.74. Fig. 109

Georges Pierre Seurat

French, 1859–91.

182 *Stone Breakers, Le Raincy* (c. 1881)

Conté crayon. 308 × 375 mm. Lillie P. Bliss Collection. 128.34.

183 *Lady with a Parasol* (1884–5)

Conté crayon. 311 × 242 mm. Abby Aldrich Rockefeller Bequest. 271.48. Fig. 2

184 *Seated Woman* (1884–5)

Conté crayon. 480 × 315 mm. Abby Aldrich Rockefeller Bequest. 272.48.

185 *At the 'Concert Européen'* (1887–8)

Conté crayon. 311 × 239 mm. Lillie P. Bliss Collection. 121.34. Fig. 3

Gino Severini

Italian, 1883–1966. To Paris 1906.

186 *Red Cross Train Passing through a Village* (1915)

Charcoal. 475 × 558 mm. Anonymous extended loan. Fig. 38

Charles Sheeler

American 1883–1965.

187 *Self-Portrait* 1923

Conté crayon, gouache, and pencil. 501 × 652 mm. Gift of Abby Aldrich Rockefeller. 146.35. Fig. 88

David Smith

American, 1906–65.

188 Untitled *(Tank Totem)* 1 August 1953

Brush and ink and gouache. 756 × 1075 mm. Gift of Alexis Gregory. 255.76. Fig. 96

Yves Tanguy

American, born France. 1900–55. To United States 1939.

189 Untitled 1947

Gouache and traces of pencil. 341 × 251 mm. The James Thrall Soby Bequest. 323.80. Fig. 80

Vladimir Tatlin

Russian, 1885–1953.

190 Study for *Board, No. 1* (1917)

Watercolour, metallic paint, gouache, and traces of pencil. 439 × 296 mm. Gift of The Lauder Foundation. 24.77. Plate IX

Fig. 1 Van Gogh *Street at Saintes-Maries* (1888) 245 × 318 mm cat. no. 53

Fig. 2 Seurat *Lady with a Parasol* (1884–85) 311 × 242 mm cat. no. 183

Fig. 3 Seurat *At the 'Concert Européen'* (1887–8) 311 × 239 mm cat. no. 185

Fig. 4 Redon *The Masque of the Red Death* (1883) 437 × 358 mm cat. no. 164

Fig. 5 Redon *The Accused* (1886) 533 × 372 mm cat. no. 166

Fig. 6 Matisse *Jeanne Manguin* (1906) 622 × 469 mm cat. no. 113

Fig. 7 Matisse *The Plumed Hat* (1919) 540 × 365 mm cat. no. 114

Fig. 8 Matisse *Reclining Nude* (1927) 277 × 320 mm cat. no. 115

Fig. 9 Matisse *Reclining Nude* 1938 605 × 813 mm cat. no. 116

Fig. 10 Matisse *Dahlias and Pomegranates* 1947 764 × 565 mm cat. no. 117

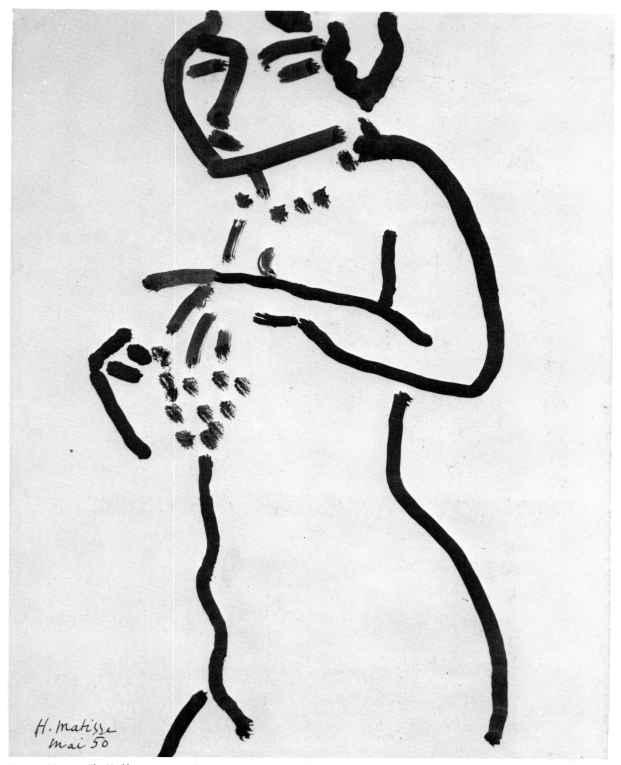

Fig. 11 Matisse *The Necklace* 1950 528 × 407 mm cat. no. 118

Fig. 12 Rouault *The Procuress* 1906 308 × 242 mm cat. no. 174

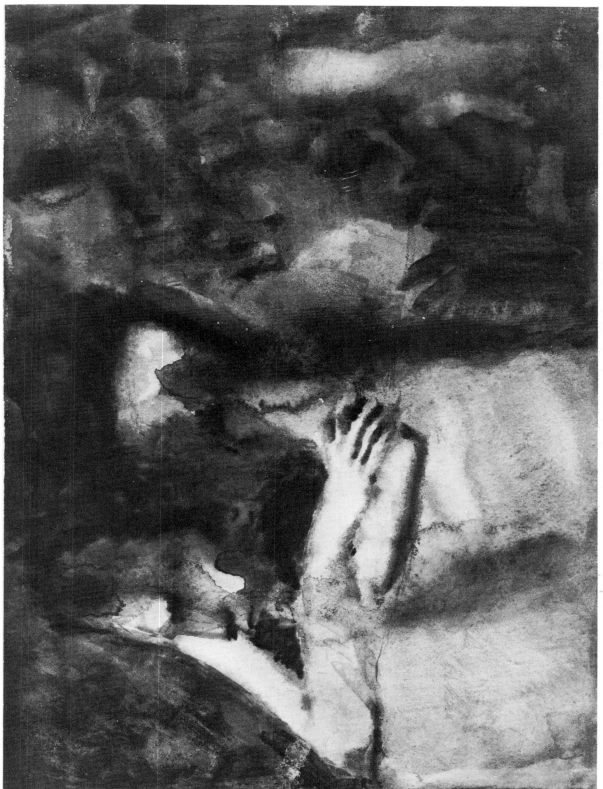

Fig. 13 Picasso *Brooding Woman* (1904) 267×366 mm cat. no. 141

Fig. 14 Picasso *Sleeping Head* (1906) 224 × 175 mm cat. no. 142

Fig. 15 Picasso *Head* (1909) 320×494 mm cat. no. 145

Fig. 16 Picasso *The Mill at Horta* (1909) 248 × 382 mm cat. no. 147

Fig. 17 Picasso *Cubist Study* (1912) 184×133 mm cat. no. 149

Fig. 18 Picasso *Study for a Construction* (1912) 172×124 mm cat. no. 150

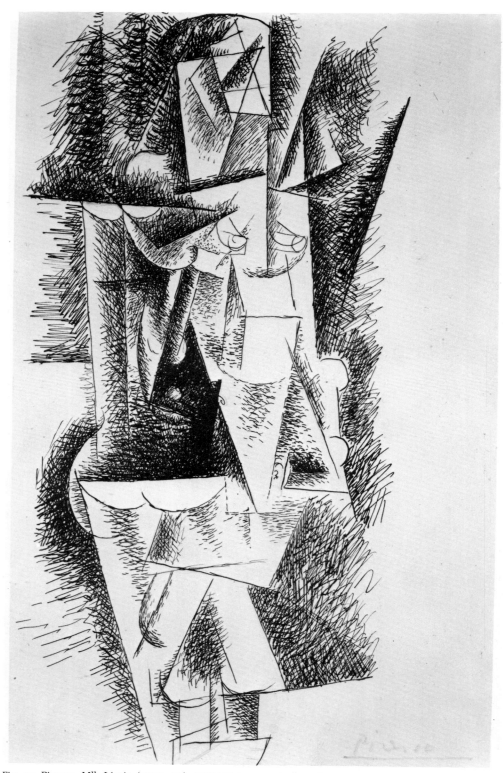

Fig. 19 Picasso *Mlle Léonie* (1911–12) 305 × 197 mm cat. no. 148

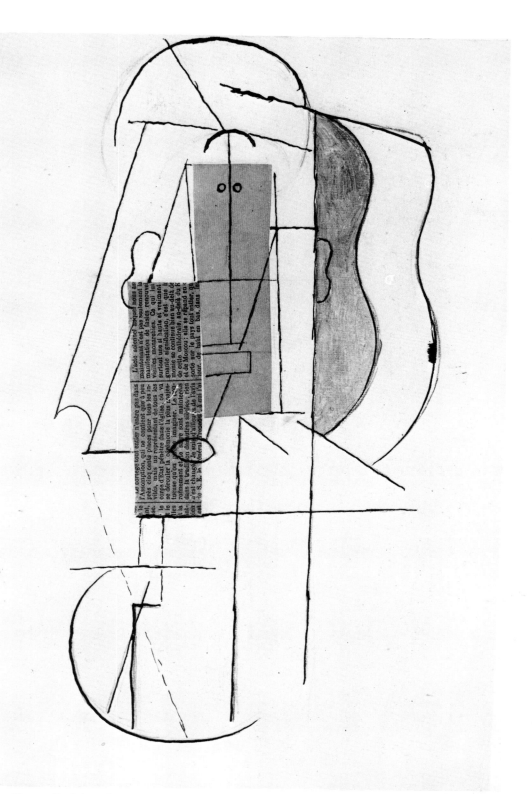

Fig. 20 Picasso *Head* (1913) 429×287 mm cat. no. 153

Fig. 21 Picasso *Man in a Melon Hat* 1914 328 × 254 mm cat. no. 154

Fig. 22 Picasso *Nessus and Dejanira* 1920 209 × 260 mm cat. no. 156

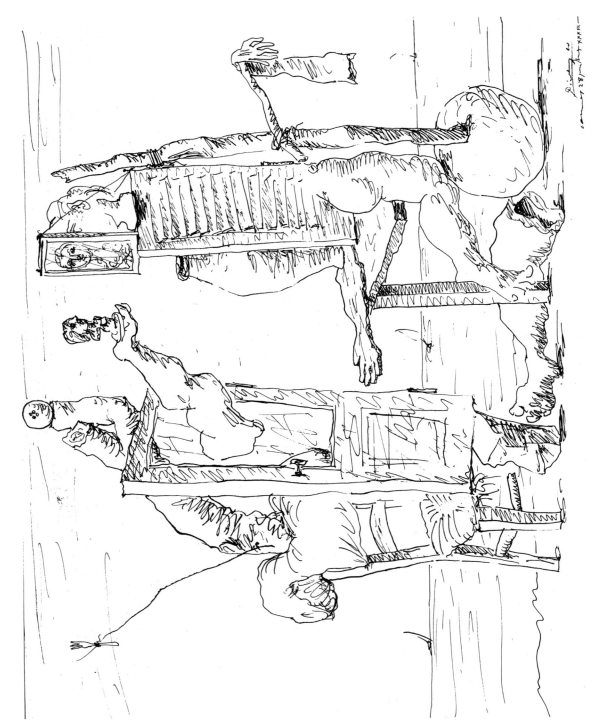

Fig. 23 Picasso *Two Figures on a Beach* 1933 400 × 508 mm cat. no. 157

Fig. 24 Delaunay *The Tower* (1911) 539×489 mm cat. no. 26

Fig. 25 Gris *Still Life with Bottle and Funnel* (1911) 479 × 316 mm cat. no. 57

Fig. 26 Picabia *New York* (1913) 558 × 759 mm cat. no. 139

Fig. 28 Atkinson *Composition* (1914) 803 × 551 mm cat. no. 6

Fig. 29 Léger *Verdun, The Trench Diggers* 1916 359 × 263 mm cat. no. 94

Fig. 30 Brancusi *The First Step* (1913) 821 × 380 mm cat. no. 14

Fig. 31 Brancusi *View of the Artist's Studio* 1918 328×411 mm cat. no. 15

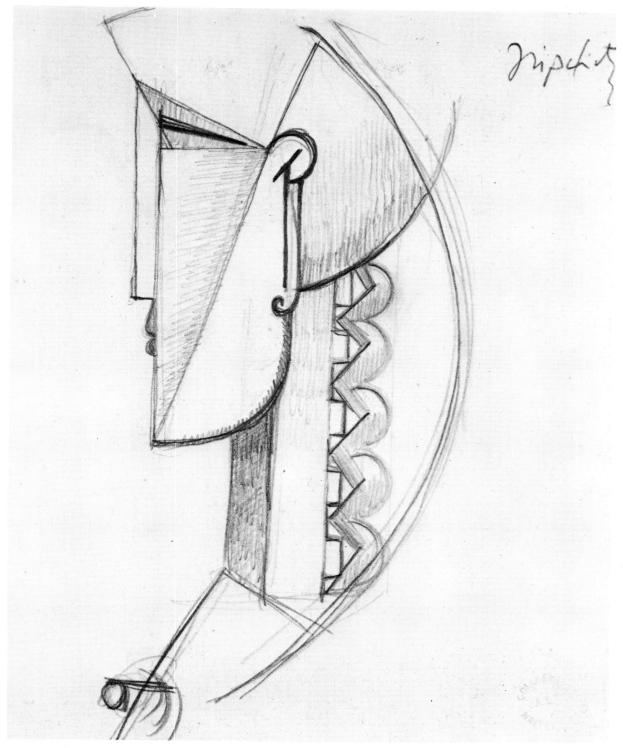

Fig. 32 Lipchitz *Girl with Braided Hair* (1914) 199×158 mm cat. no. 100

Fig. 33 Modigliani *Seated Nude* (1914) 540×416 mm cat. no. 126

Fig. 34 Giacometti *Head of a Woman* 1923 302×230 mm cat. no. 52

Fig. 35 Balla Study for *A Street Light* (1909) 220 × 180 mm cat. no. 8

Fig. 36 Carra *Ritmi Plastici* 1911 107 × 740 mm cat. no. 17

Fig. 37 Boccioni *States of Mind: The Farewells* (1911) 584 × 863 mm cat. no. 13

Fig. 38 Severini *Red Cross Train Passing through a Village* (1915) 475 × 558 mm cat. no. 186

Fig. 39 Chagall *Golgotha* 1912 474×592 mm cat. no. 22

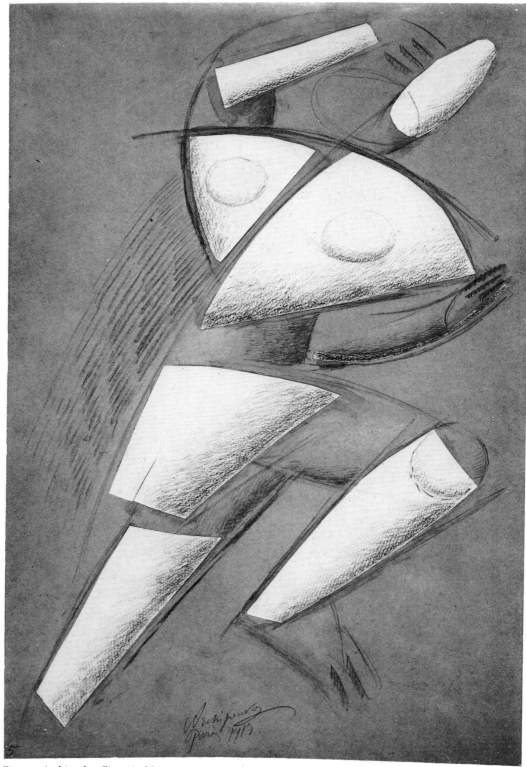

Fig. 40 Archipenko *Figure in Movement* 1913 476 × 314 mm cat. no. 3

Fig. 41 Malevich *Suprematist Elements: Squares* (1915) 502 × 358 mm cat. no. 105

Fig. 42 Rozanova *The Universal War* 1916 cat. no. 175

Fig. 43 Rodchenko *Composition* 1918
330×162 mm cat. no. 168

Fig. 44 Lissitzky Study for page for *A Suprematist Story* (1920) 256 × 202 mm cat. no. 102

Fig. 45 Mondrian *Church Facade* (1914) 990×634 mm cat. no. 128

Fig. 47 Mondrian Study for *Broadway
Boogie Woogie II* 229 × 232 mm
cat. no. 130

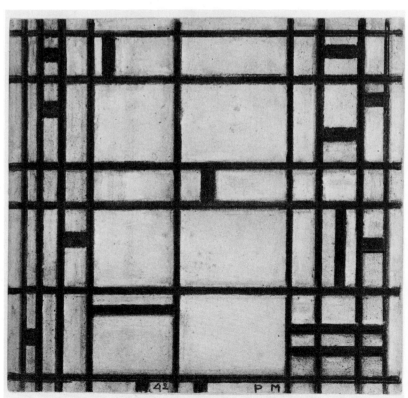

Fig. 46 Mondrian Study for *Broadway
Boogie Woogie* 1942 229 × 232 mm
cat. no. 129

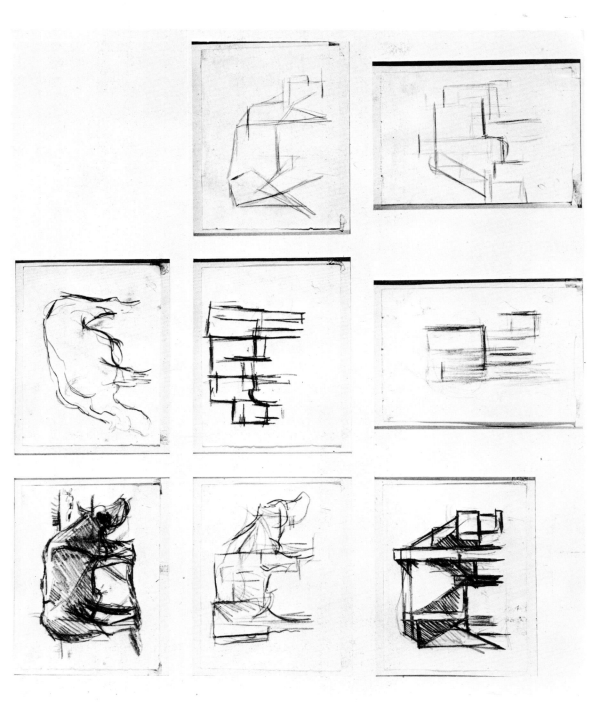

Fig. 48 Van Doesburg Eight studies for *Composition (The Cow)* (1916) cat. no. 35

Fig. 49 Van Doesburg *Composition (The Cow)* 1916 397×577 mm cat. no. 36

Fig. 50 Van der Leck Untitled (1917) 447×571 mm cat. no. 93

Fig. 51 Marc *Blue Horse with Rainbow* (1913) 162 × 257 mm cat. no. 107

Fig. 52 Kandinsky Study for *Painting with White Form* (1913) 276 × 381 mm cat. no. 71

Fig. 53 Feininger *Ruin by the Sea, II* 1934 302×490 mm cat. no. 49

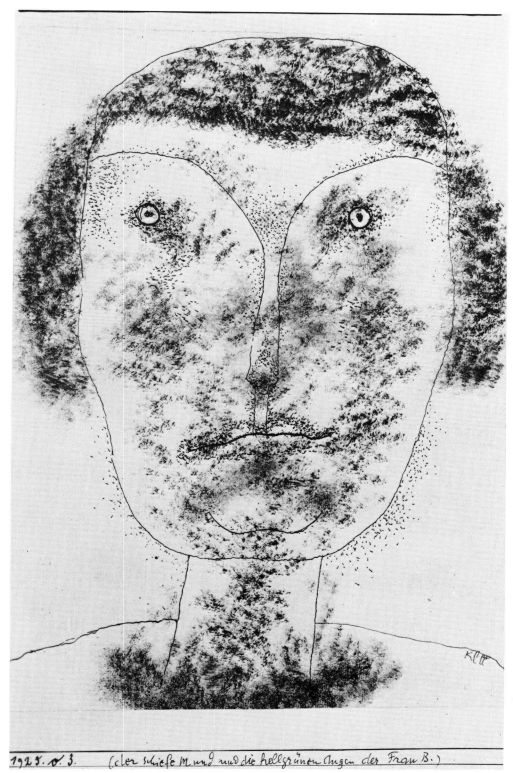

1925. N. 3. (der schiefe Mund und die hellgrünen Augen der Frau B.)

Fig. 54 Klee *The Crooked Mouth and Light Green Eyes of Mrs B.* 1925 165 × 362 mm cat. no. 79

Fig. 55 Klee *Lady Apart* 1940 416 × 295 mm cat. no. 84

Fig. 56 Kokoschka *Nude with Back* (1907) 451 × 311 mm cat. no. 86

Fig. 57 Heckel *Girl Reading (Young Girl)* 1912 502 × 335 mm cat. no. 64

Fig. 58 Kirchner *Street Scene, Berlin* (1914) 546 × 394 mm cat. no. 76

Fig. 59 Nolde *Magicians* (1931–5) 511 × 365 mm cat. no. 134

Fig. 60 Dix *Café Couple* 1921 508 × 410 mm cat. no. 34

Fig. 61 Beckman *The Return of the Prodigal Son* (1921) 364×298 mm cat. no. 11

Fig. 62 Grosz *Dispute by Moonlight* (1920) 676 × 498 mm cat. no. 60

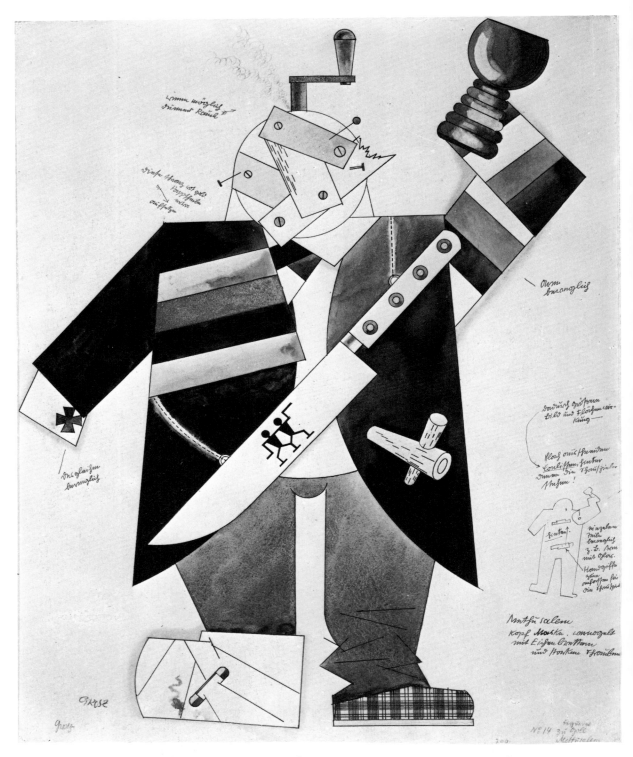

Fig. 63 Grosz *Methuselah* (1922) 526 × 411 mm cat. no. 62

Fig. 64 Grosz *Circe* 1927 660×486 mm cat. no. 63

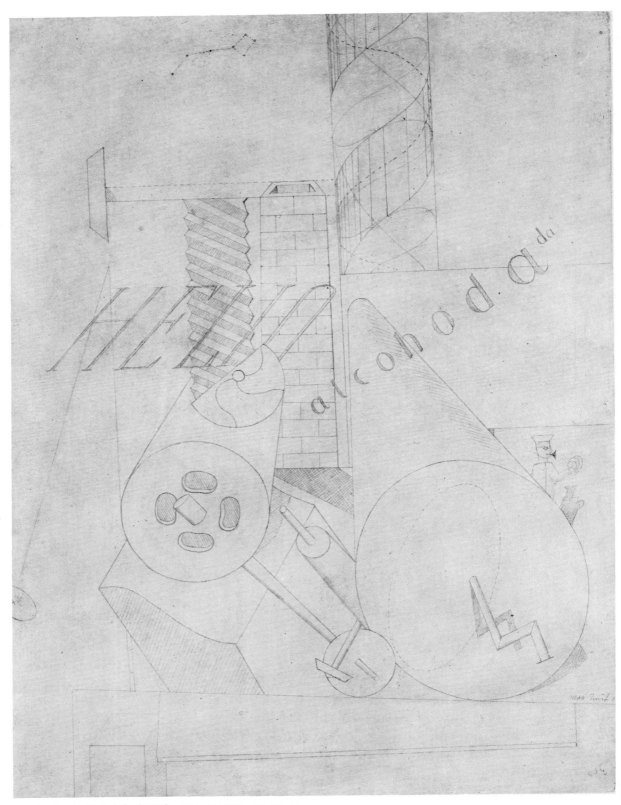

Fig. 65 Ernst *Alcohodada* (1919) 449 × 334 mm cat. no. 44

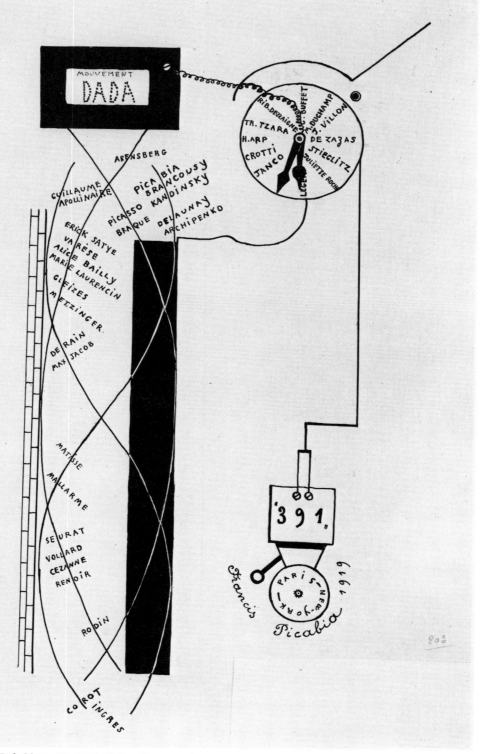

Fig. 66 Picabia *Dada Movement* 1919 511 × 362 mm cat. no. 140

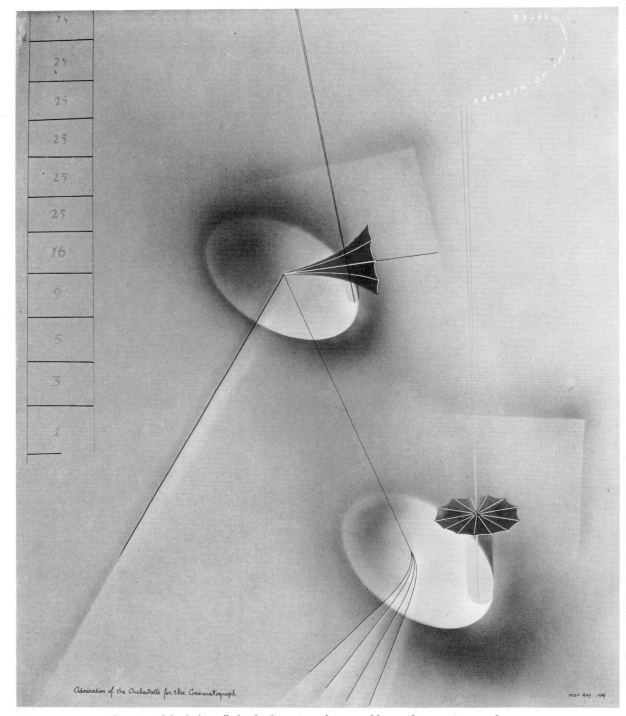

Fig. 67 Man Ray *Admiration of the Orchestrelle for the Cinematograph* 1919 660 × 546 mm cat. no. 106

Fig. 68 Moholy-Nagy *Chute* 1923 648×495 mm cat. no. 127

Fig. 69 Hoch *Man and Machine* (1921) 290 × 242 mm cat. no. 65

Fig. 70 Schlemmer Study for *The Triadic Ballet* (1921–3) 575 × 371 mm cat. no. 177

Fig. 71 Ernst *Here Everything Is Still Floating* (1920) 105 × 124 mm cat. no. 45

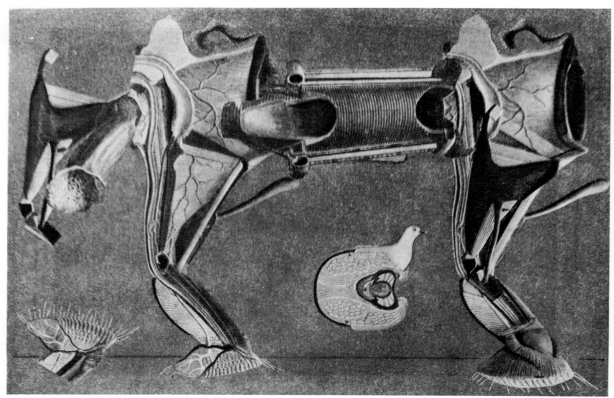

Fig. 72 Ernst *The Horse, He's Sick* (1920) 146 × 216 mm cat. no. 46

PLATE I Van Gogh *Hospital Corridor at Saint-Remy* (1889) 613 × 473 mm cat. no. 54.

PLATE II *Cézanne Foliage* (1895–1900) 448 × 568 mm cat. no. 20.

PLATE III Derain *Three Dancers* (*Bacchic Dance*) (1906) 495 × 648 mm cat. no. 29.

PLATE IV Picasso *Head of the Medical Student* (1907) 603 × 470 mm cat. no. 143.

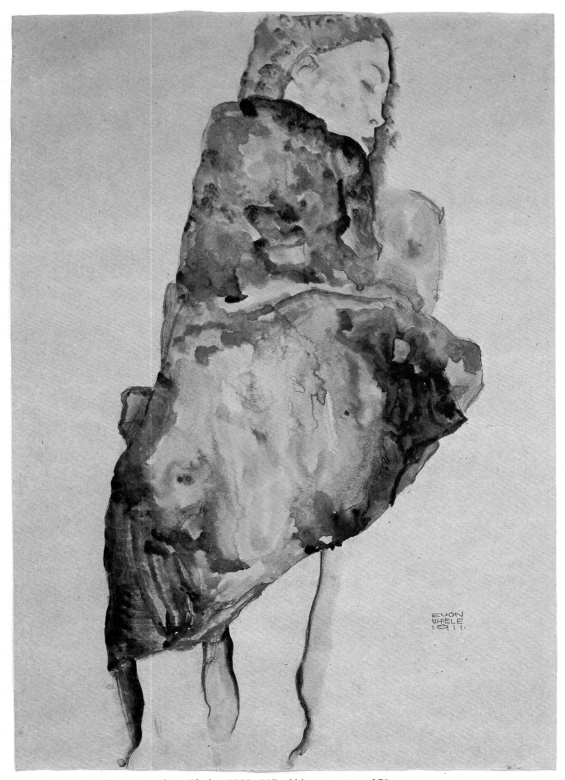

PLATE V Schiele *Woman Wrapped in a Blanket* 1911 447 × 311 mm cat. no. 176.

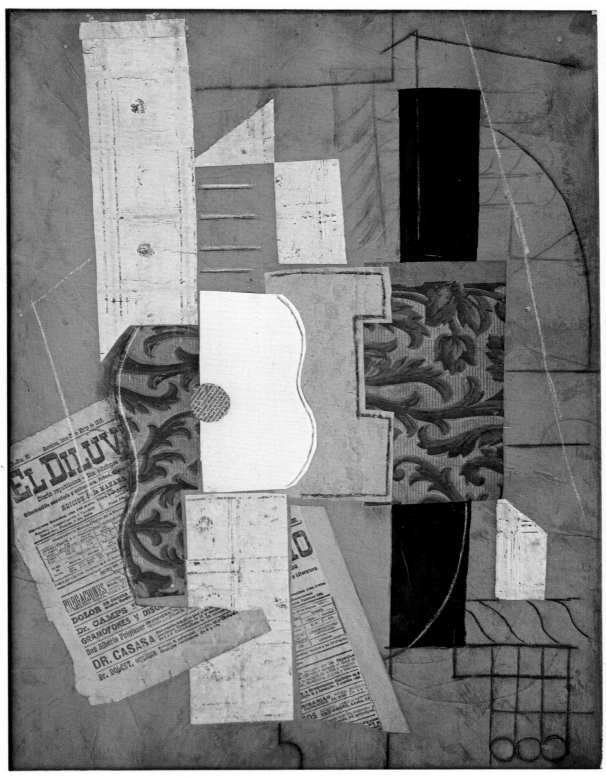

PLATE VI Picasso *Guitar* 1913 664 × 496 mm cat. no. 152.

PLATE VII Gris *Breakfast* (1914) 809 × 597 mm cat. no. 58.

PLATE VIII Klee *Laughing Gothic*
1915 260 × 136 mm
cat. no. 77.

PLATE IX Tatlin *Study for Board No. 1* (1917) 439 × 296 mm cat. no. 190.

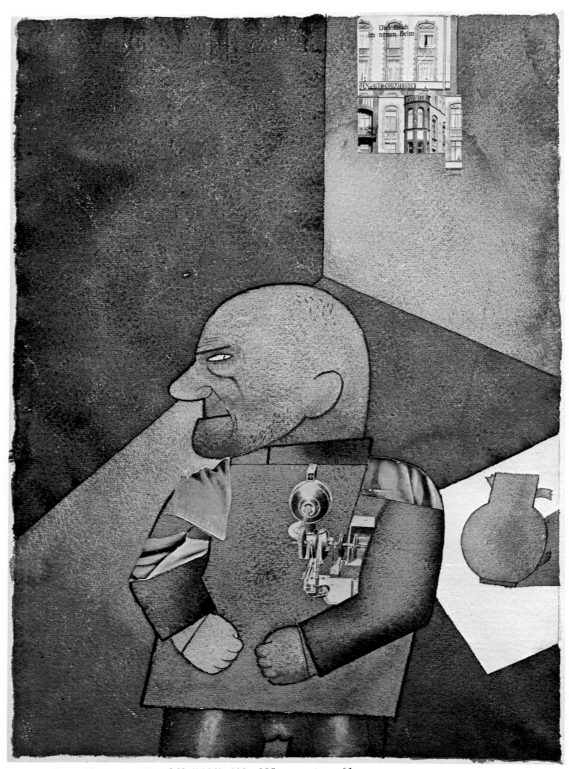

PLATE X Grosz *The Engineer Heartfield* (1920) 419 × 305 mm cat. no. 61.

PLATE XI Schwitters *Merz: Santa Claus* 1922 284 × 208 mm cat. no. 180.

PLATE XII Kandinsky *Black Relationship* 1924 368 × 362 mm cat. no. 74.

PLATE XIII Miró *The Beautiful Bird Revealing the Unknown to a Pair of Lovers* 1941 457 × 381 mm cat. no. 124.

PLATE XIV De Kooning *Standing Woman* (1952) 303 × 241 mm cat. no. 87.

PLATE XV Pollock *Untitled* (1951) 615 × 864 mm cat. no. 161.

PLATE XVI Rauschenberg *Dante's Inferno*, Canto XXXI: The Central Pit of Malbolge, The Giants (1959–60) 368 × 291 mm
cat. no. 163.

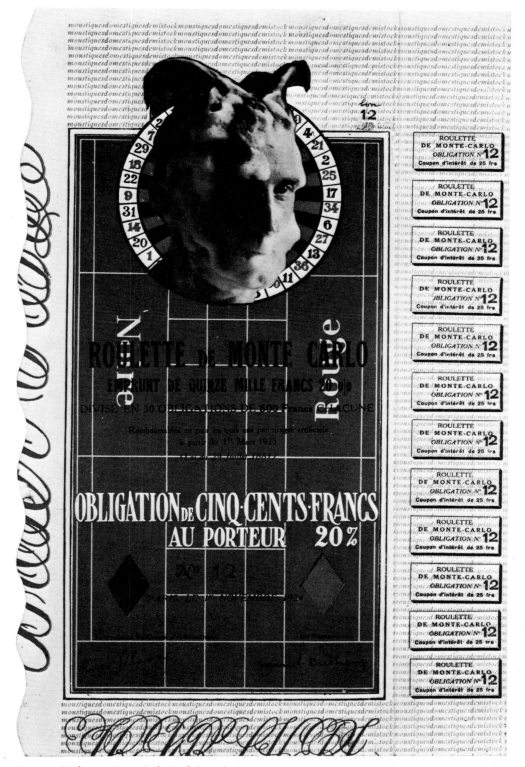

Fig. 73 Duchamp *Monte Carlo Bond* (1924) 311 × 197 mm cat. no. 42

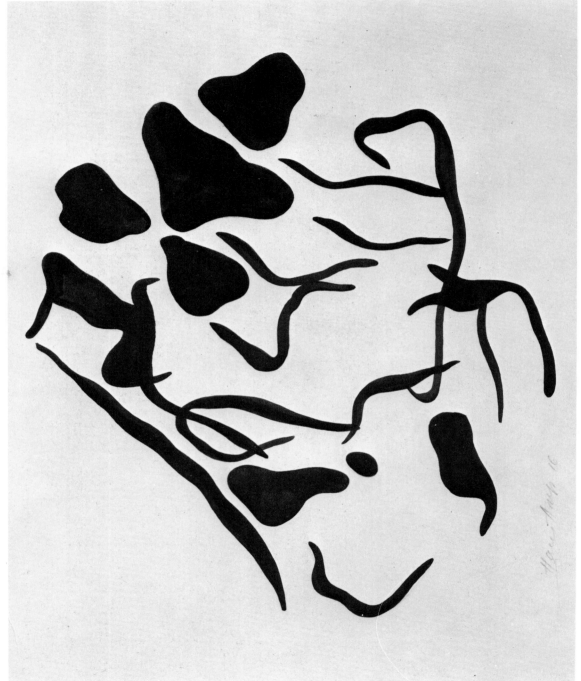

Fig. 74 Arp *Automatic Drawing* 1916 426 × 540 mm cat. no. 4

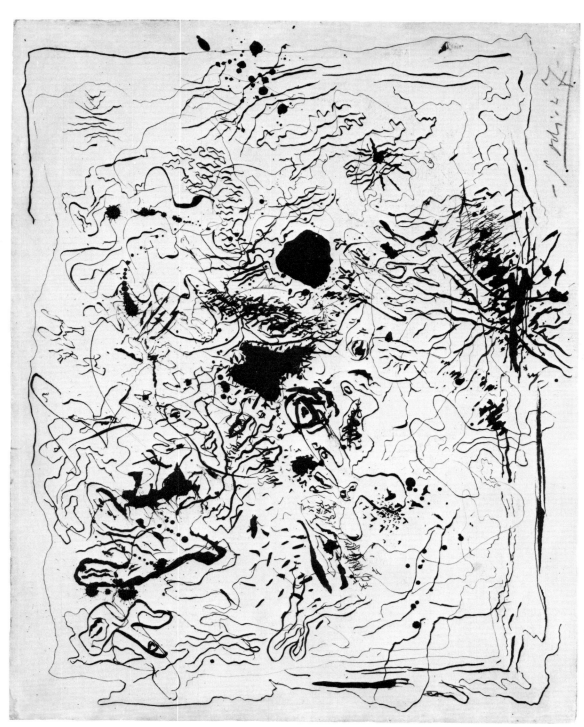

Fig. 75 Dali Untitled 1927 251 × 326 mm cat. no. 24

Fig. 76 Exquisite Corpse (composite drawing) Untitled (1935) 276 × 208 mm cat. no. 48

Fig. 77 Dominguez Untitled 1936 359 × 252 mm cat. no. 37

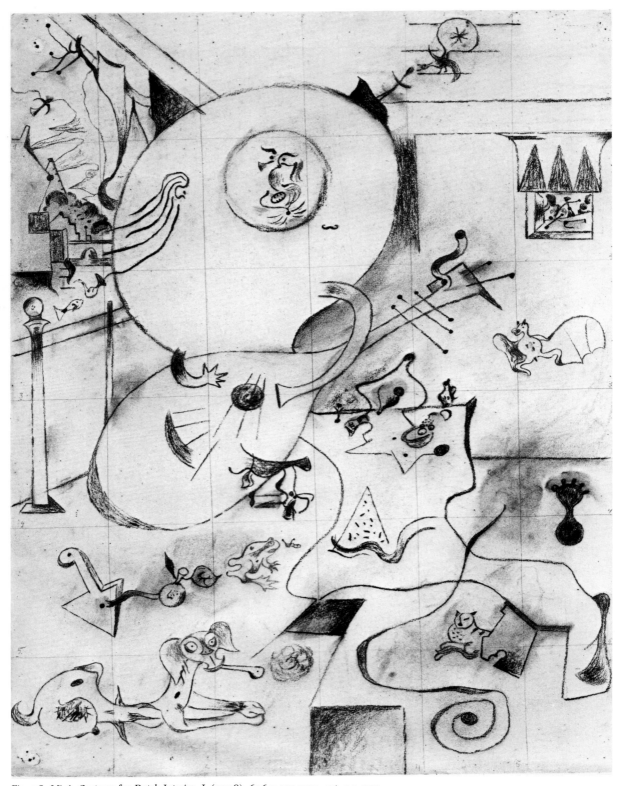

Fig. 78 Miró Cartoon for *Dutch Interior, I* (1928) 626 × 473 mm cat. no. 121

Fig. 79 Miró *Collage* 1934 369 × 236 mm cat. no. 123

Fig. 80 Tanguy Untitled 1947 341 × 251 mm cat. no. 189

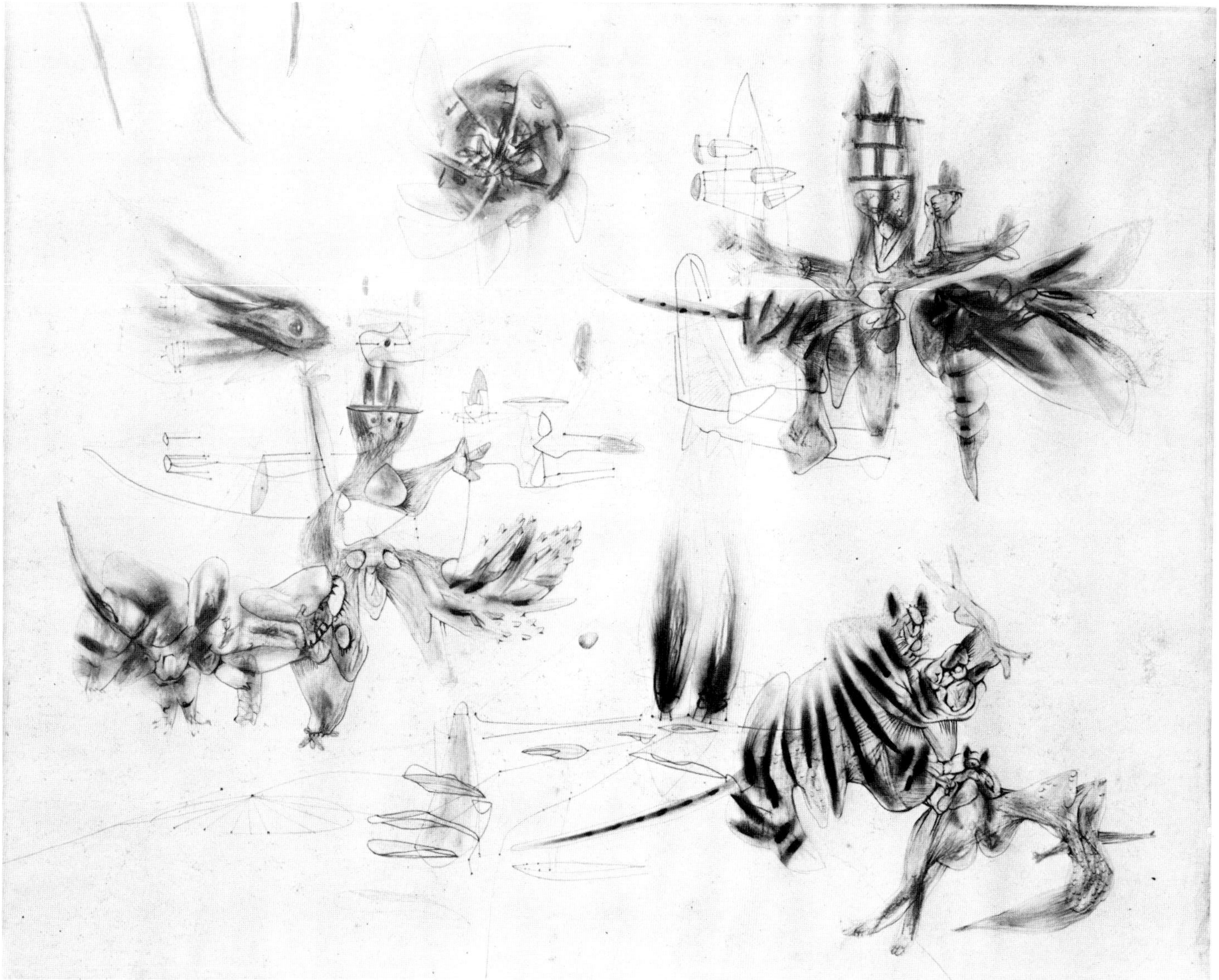

Fig. 81 Matta Untitled 1942 486 × 612 mm cat. no. 119

Fig. 82 Masson *Werewolf* (1944) 457×610 mm cat. no. 112

Fig. 83 Dubuffet *Joe Bousquet in Bed* 1947 494 × 323 mm cat. no. 38

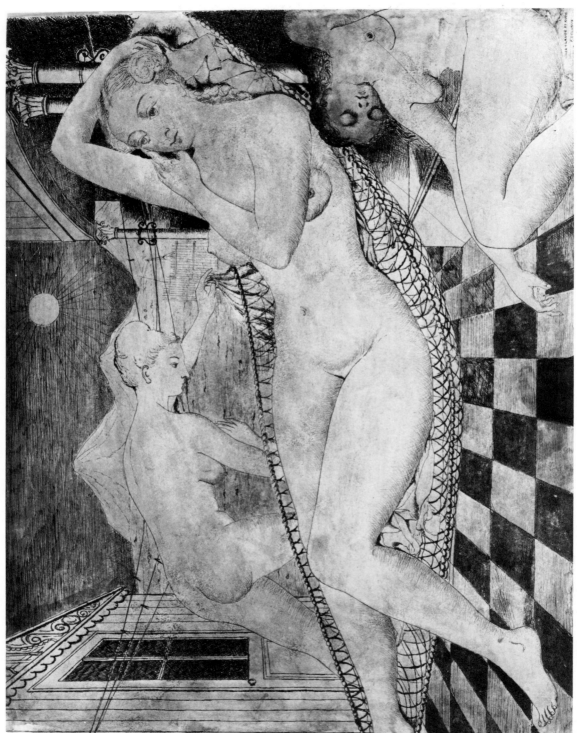

Fig. 84 Delvaux *The Siesta* 1947 595 × 783 mm cat. no. 28

Fig. 85 Moore *Women Winding Wool* 1949 348×636 mm cat. no. 131

Fig. 86 Marin *Lower Manhattan (Composing Derived from Top of Woolworth)* 1922 549 × 683 mm
cat. no. 108

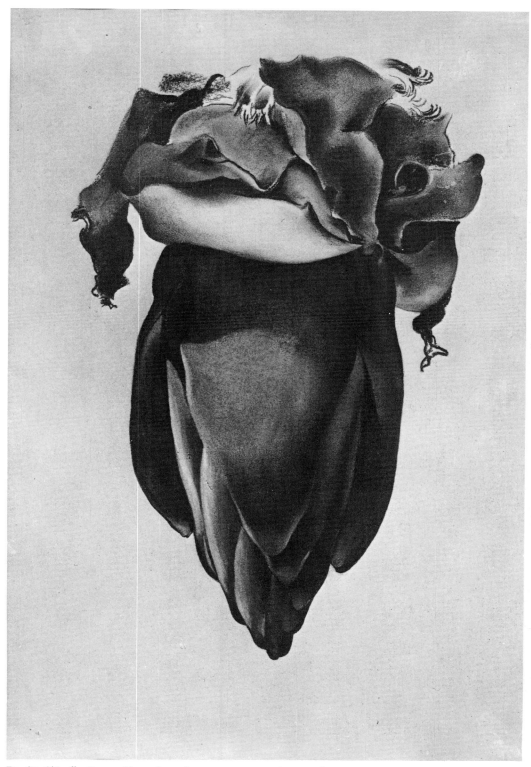

Fig. 87 O'Keeffe *Banana Flower* (1933) 552 × 357 mm cat. no. 136

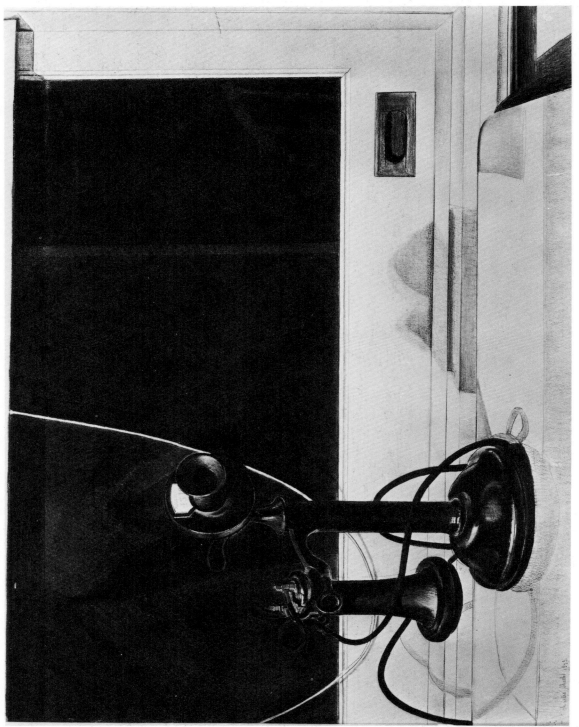

Fig. 88 Sheeler *Self-Portrait* 1923 501×652 mm cat. no. 187

Fig. 89 Hopper *Box Factory, Gloucester* (1928) 356 × 508 mm cat. no. 66

Fig. 90 Davis *Composition No. 5* (1932) 559 × 759 mm cat. no. 25

Fig. 91 Léger *Face and Hands* 1952 660×501 mm cat. no. 96

Fig. 92 Gorky *Portrait of Vartoosh* (1935) 312 × 241 mm cat. no. 55

Fig. 93 Gorky *Study for Summation* 1946 470×618 mm cat. no. 56

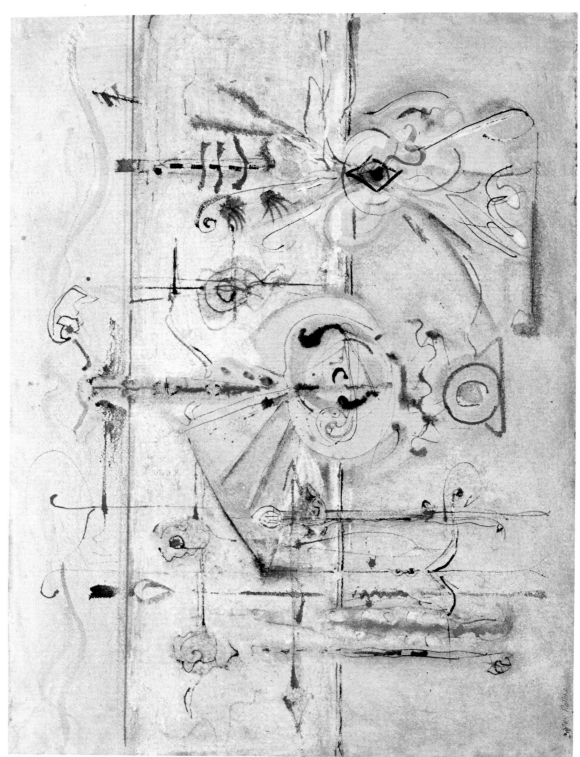

Fig. 94 Rothko *Archaic Idol* (1945) 556 × 762 mm cat. no. 172

Fig. 95 Pollock Untitled (c. 1950) 444×565 mm cat. no. 159

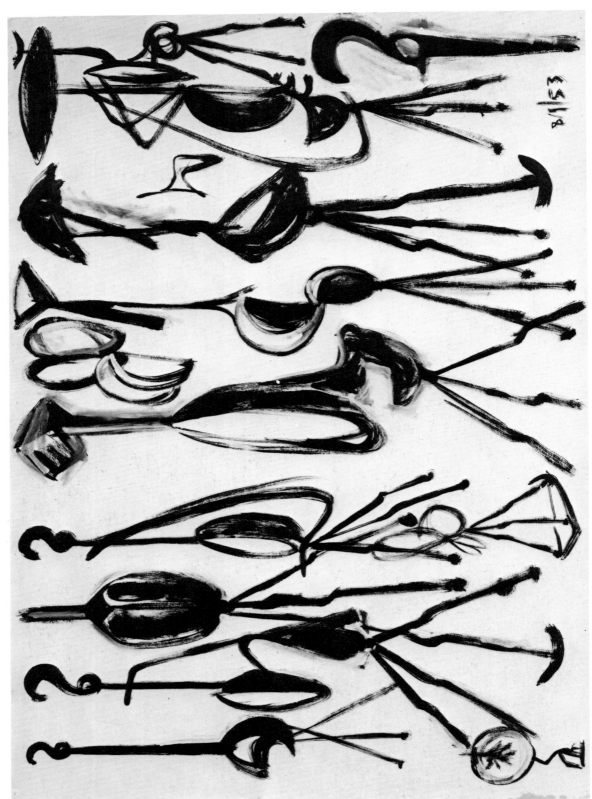

Fig. 96 Smith Untitled (*Tank Totem*) 1953 756 × 1075 mm cat. no. 188

Fig. 97 Francis Untitled (1958) 687 × 1017 mm cat. no. 50

Fig. 98 Rauschenberg Canto IV from 34 illustrations for Dante's *Inferno* (1959–60). Limbo, Circle I. The Virtuous Pagans 368 × 291 mm cat. no. 163

Fig. 99 Rauschenberg Canto XIV from 34 illustrations for Dante's *Inferno* (1959–60). Circle 7, Round 3. The Violent Against God, Nature and Art 368 × 291 mm cat. no. 163

Fig. 100 Dine *Five-bladed Saw* (from *Seven Untitled Drawings*) 1973 651 × 502 mm cat. no. 30

Fig. 101 Dine *Second Baby Drawing* 1976 1011×775 mm cat. no. 33

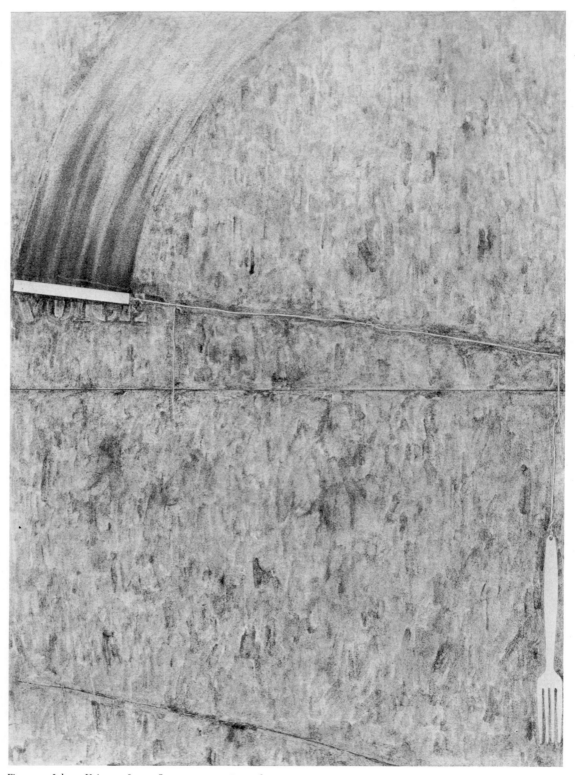

Fig. 102 Johns *Voice* 1969 718×521 mm cat. no. 69

Fig. 103 Johns *Savarin* 1977 921 × 664 mm cat. no. 70

Fig. 104 Oldenburg Preliminary study for *Image of the Buddha Preaching* 1967 764 × 561 mm cat. no. 138

Fig. 105 Balthus *Reclining Nude* (1967) 500 × 698 mm cat. no. 9

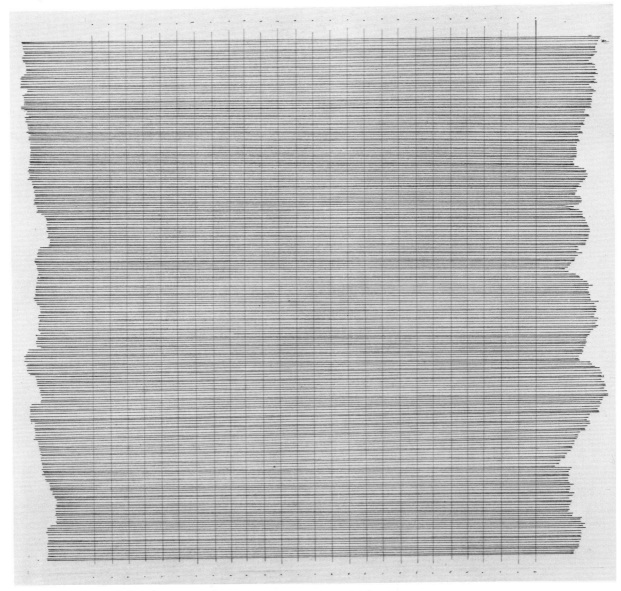

Fig. 106 Martin Untitled 1960 302 × 306 mm cat. no. 109

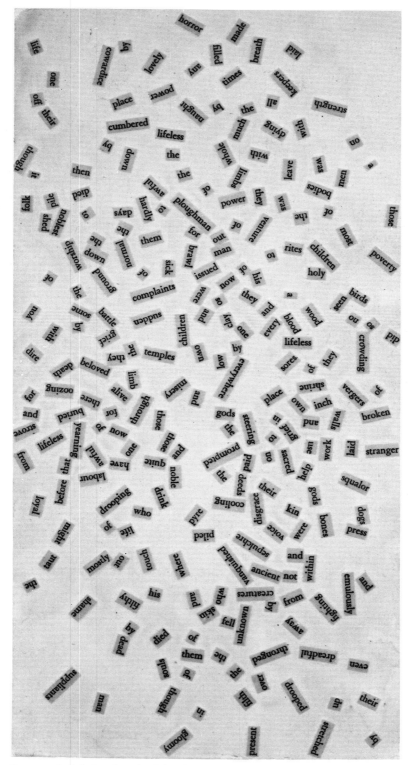

Fig. 107 André *Crowding* (1965) 285 × 143 mm cat. no. 1

PLAN FOR WALL DRAWING / PAULA COOPER GALLERY / MAY 15,16 1969

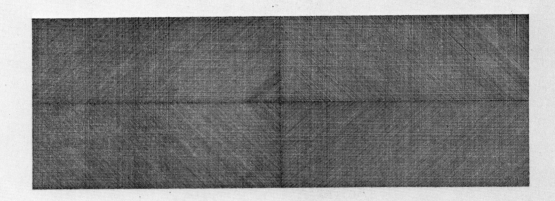

The wall drawing was executed by Adrian Piper, Henry Otter and Sol LeWitt on the south
wall of the smaller room of the Paula Cooper Gallery, 96 Prince St. It is part of an
exhibition for the benefit of the Art Workers Coalition and was compiled by Lucy Lippard.
This drawing is 16'6" X 6', composed of four sections, each 4'4" X 3', and was drawn with
9H graphite sticks. The drawing is the width of the wall, the height of each section 3')
is dictated by the maximum length that a line can be easily drawn using a 45°
right triangle as a guide. Each of the four sections has three crossing lines superimposed on one another (vertical, horizontal, diagonal left to right, and diagonal
right to left - 45°), representing the basic directions that lines can be drawn. These
lines are drawn as lightly and as close together as possible (½"). The tonality
of the drawing should be equal since there are an equal number of lines in each
segment. However the properties of the wall, in some cases, dictate the darkness
of the lines & if there is a trace of grease or foreign substance, or if the wall bulges
out). The pressure exerted by the draftsmen is not always equal, nor is the
distance between lines always the same accounting for darker areas. These
deviations are acceptable and beyond the scope of planning, they are inherent in the
method. The wall drawing is perceived first as a light tonal mass - light enough
to preserve the integrity of the wall plane - and then as a collection of lines. Neither
the wall drawing, this drawing in ink, or the photographic record of the wall drawing
are definitive but all are of equal importance. The wall drawing is temporary
and will be removed at the discretion of the Paula Cooper Gallery. Sol LeWitt May 20,1969

Fig. 108 LeWitt *Plan for Wall Drawing* 1969 527×526 mm cat. no. 97

Fig. 109 Serra *Heir* (1973) 2912 × 1072 mm cat. no. 181

Fig. 110 Morris *Blind Time XIII* 1973 892 × 1172 mm cat. no. 132

Fig. 111 Rockburne *Copal No. 8* 1976 740×994 mm cat. no. 167

Fig. 112 Nauman *Face Mask* 1981 1340×1778 mm cat. no. 133